MW01119720

Western European Perspectives on the Development of Public Relations

DOI: 10.1057/9781137427519.0001

National Perspectives on the Development of Public Relations

Series Editor: **Tom Watson**, Professor of Public Relations, The Media School
Bournemouth University, UK

The history of public relations has long been presented in a corporatist Anglo-American framework. The National Perspectives on the Development of Public Relations: Other Voices series is the first to offer an authentic world-wide view of the history of public relations freed from those influences.

The series will feature six books, five of which cover continental and regional groups including (Book 1) Asia and Australasia, (Book 2) Eastern Europe and Russia, (Book 3) Middle East and Africa, (Book 4) Latin America and Caribbean and (Book 5) Western Europe. The sixth book will have essays on new and revised historiographical and theoretical approaches.

Written by leading national public relations historians and scholars, some histories of national public relations development are offered for the first time while others are reinterpreted in a more authentic style. *The National Perspectives on the Development of Public Relations: Other Voices* series makes a major contribution to the wider knowledge of PR's history and aids formation of new historiographical and theoretical approaches.

Titles include:

Tom Watson (*editor*)
WESTERN EUROPEAN PERSPECTIVES ON THE DEVELOPMENT OF PUBLIC RELATIONS
Other Voices

Tom Watson (*editor*)
LATIN AMERICAN AND CARIBBEAN PERSPECTIVES ON THE DEVELOPMENT OF PUBLIC RELATIONS
Other Voices

Tom Watson (*editor*)
MIDDLE EASTERN AND AFRICAN PERSPECTIVES ON THE DEVELOPMENT OF PUBLIC RELATIONS
Other Voices

Tom Watson (*editor*)
EASTERN EUROPEAN PERSPECTIVES ON THE DEVELOPMENT OF PUBLIC RELATIONS
Other Voices

Tom Watson (*editor*)
ASIAN PERSPECTIVES ON THE DEVELOPMENT OF PUBLIC RELATIONS
Other Voices

National Perspectives on the Development of Public Relations
Series Standing Order ISBN 978–1–137–39811–6 hardback
(*outside North America only*)

You can receive future titles in this series as they are published by placing a standing order. Please contact your bookseller or, in case of difficulty, write to us at the address below with your name and address, the title of the series and the ISBN quoted above.

Customer Services Department, Macmillan Distribution Ltd, Houndmills, Basingstoke, Hampshire RG21 6XS, England.

DOI: 10.1057/9781137427519.0001

palgrave▸pivot

Western European Perspectives on the Development of Public Relations: Other Voices

Edited by

Tom Watson
Professor of Public Relations, Faculty of Media &
Communication, Bournemouth University

▸

palgrave
macmillan

DOI: 10.1057/9781137427519.0001

First published 2015 by
PALGRAVE MACMILLAN

Palgrave Macmillan in the UK is an imprint of Macmillan Publishers Limited,
registered in England, company number 785998, of Houndmills, Basingstoke,
Hampshire RG21 6XS.

Palgrave Macmillan in the US is a division of St Martin's Press LLC,
175 Fifth Avenue, New York, NY 10010.

Palgrave Macmillan is the global academic imprint of the above companies
and has companies and representatives throughout the world.

Palgrave® and Macmillan® are registered trademarks in the United States,
the United Kingdom, Europe and other countries.

ISBN: 978-1-137-42750-2 EPUB
ISBN: 978-1-137-42751-9 PDF
ISBN: 978-1-137-42749-6 Hardback

A catalogue record for this book is available from the British Library.

A catalog record for this book is available from the Library of Congress.

www.palgrave.com/pivot

DOI: 10.1057/9781137427519

This series is dedicated to my wife, Jenny, who has endured three decades of my practice and research in public relations ('I'll be finished soon' has been my response to her on too many occasions), and to the scholars and practitioners who have embraced and contributed so much to the International History of Public Relations Conference. They have come to Bournemouth University each year from around the world and reinvigorated the scholarship of public relations history. I hope everyone enjoys this series and are inspired to develop their research.

Tom Watson

DOI: 10.1057/9781137427519.0001

Contents

DOI: 10.1057/9781137427519.0001

DOI: 10.1057/9781137427519.0001

Series Editor's Preface

This series will make a major contribution to the history and historiography of public relations (PR). Until recently publications and conference papers have focused mainly on American tropes that PR was invented in the United States, although there have been British and German challenges to this claim. There are, however, emerging narratives that public relations-type activity developed in many countries in other bureaucratic and cultural forms that only came in contact with Anglo-American practice recently.

The scholarship of public relations has largely been driven by US perspectives with a limited level of research undertaken in the United Kingdom and Central Europe. This has been reflected in general PR texts, which mostly tell the story of PR's development from the US experience. Following the establishment of the International History of Public Relations Conference (IHPRC), first held in 2010, it is evident there is an increasing level of research, reflection and scholarship outside Anglo-America and Central European orbits.

From IHPRC and a recent expansion of publishing in public relations academic journals, new national perspectives on the formation of public relations structures and practices are being published and discussed. Some reflect Anglo-American influences while others have evolved from national cultural and communication practices with a sideways glace at international practices.

I am attached to the notion of 'other' both in its postmodern concept and as a desire to create a more authentic approach to the history of public relations. It was the UK

DOI: 10.1057/9781137427519.0002

public relations scholar and historian Professor Jacquie L'Etang who first used 'the other' in discussion with me. It immediately encapsulated my concerns about some recent historical writing, especially from countries outside Western Europe and North America. There was much evidence that 'Western hegemonic public relations' was influencing authors to make their national histories conform to the primacy of the United States. Often it was processed through the four models of Grunig and Hunt (1984). This approach did not take account of the social, cultural and political forces that formed each nation's approach to PR. It was also dull reading.

National Perspectives on the Development of Public Relations: Other Voices will be the first series to bring forward these different, sometimes alternative and culturally diverse national histories of public relations in a single format. Some will be appearing for the first time. In this series, national narratives are introduced and discussed, enabling the development of new or complementary theories on the establishment of public relations around the world.

Overall, the series has three aims:

1   Introduce national perspectives on the formation of public relations practices and structures in countries outside Western Europe and North America;
2   Challenge existing US-centric modelling of public relations;
3   Aid the formation of new knowledge and theory on the formation of public relations practices and structures by offering accessible publications of high quality.

Five of the books will focus on national public relations narratives which are collected together on a continental basis: Asia and Australasia, Eastern Europe and Russia, Middle East and Africa, Latin America and Caribbean, and Western Europe. The sixth book addresses historiographic interpretations and theorization of public relations history.

Rather than requesting authors to write in a prescribed format which leaves little flexibility, they have been encouraged to research and write historical narratives and analysis that are pertinent to a particular country or region. My view is that a national historical account of public relations' evolution will be more prized and exciting to read if the author is encouraged to present a narrative of how it developed over one or more particular periods (determined by what is appropriate in that country), considering why one or two particular PR events or persons

DOI: 10.1057/9781137427519.0002

(or none) were important in that country, reviewing cultural traditions and interpretations of historical experiences, and theorizing development of public relations into its present state. Chapters without enforced consistency to the structure and focus have enabled the perspectives and voices from the different countries to be told in a way that is relevant to their histories.

A more original discussion follows in the concluding book because the series editor and fellow contributors offer a more insightful commentary on the historical development in the regions, identifying a contextualized emergent theoretical framework and historiography that values differences, rather than attempting to 'test' an established theoretical framework or historiographic approach.

Tom Watson
twatson@bournemouth.ac.uk

Reference

Grunig, J. and Hunt, T. (1984) *Managing Public Relations* (New York: Holt, Rinehart and Winston).

DOI: 10.1057/9781137427519.0002

Notes on Contributors

Tom Watson is Professor of Public Relations in the Faculty of Media & Communication at Bournemouth University, United Kingdom. Before entering academic life, Tom's career covered journalism and public relations in Australia, the United Kingdom and internationally. He ran a successful public relations consultancy in England for 18 years and was chairman of the United Kingdom's Public Relations Consultants Association from 2000 to 2002. Tom's research focuses on professionally-important topics such as measurement and evaluation, reputation management, and corporate social responsibility. He also researches and writes on public relations history and established the annual International History of Public Relations Conference in 2010. Tom is a Fellow of the Chartered Institute of Public Relations and a Founding Fellow of the Public Relations Consultants Association. Tom took his first degree at the University of New South Wales in 1974. He was awarded his PhD in 1995 (Nottingham Trent University) for research into models of evaluation in public relations, edits the annual Public Relations History special issue of *Public Relations Review* and is on the editorial board of several other journals.

Tor Bang, PhD, is Associate Professor in the Department of Communication and Culture at the BI Norwegian Business School in Oslo.

Günter Bentele, Dr Phil., is Professor emeritus for Public Relations at the University of Leipzig. He held the first Chair for Public Relations (Öffentlichkeitsarbeit/PR) in the German-speaking countries from 1994 until his retirement in fall 2014. Bentele is author, co-author, editor and co-editor of some 40 books and more than 180 scientific articles in the fields of public relations, communication theory, journalism and semiotics, as well as editor of two book series. In 2004, he was President of EUPRERA and also honoured as 'PR personality of the year' by DPRG (German Public Relations Association).

Valérie Carayol is Professor in the Department of Communication Studies at Bordeaux Montaigne University (France). She is the director of the MICA research group (69 academic full members, 100 doctoral students) and editor of the academic review *Communication and Organisation*, published by the University of Bordeaux Press (PUB), and a former President of EUPRERA (2011–2014). Her publications include six scholarly books and numerous articles, book chapters, reviews and papers.

Bruno Chaudet, PhD, is Associate Professor at the University of Rennes 2 (PREFics research group – EA 4246), and is Head of Professional Relations for the French Information and Communications Science Society (SFSIC). He worked for ten years as PR officer for a public administration coordinating social housing, before presenting his PhD on collaborative platforms and process logics in the social housing sector.

Anne-Marie Cotton holds a Master's in Romance Philology (Ghent University, Belgium), Business Administration (Lille University, France) and Marketing (Vlerick School of Business Leuven-Ghent, Belgium). She is Senior Lecturer in Communication Studies at Arteveldehogeschool University College (Ghent, Belgium) and coordinates the Master's in European Public Relations (MARPE). She has been President of EUPRERA.

Alex Frame, PhD, is Associate Professor in Communications at the University of Burgundy (Dijon) where he works within the TIL research group (EA4182). His research is centred on intercultural, political and organizational communications/PR, and notably the use of Twitter and social networks within these areas.

Finn Frandsen is Professor of Corporate Communication and Director of Center for Corporate Communication (CCC) in the School of Business and Social Sciences, Aarhus University (Denmark). The institutionalization of strategic communication in private and public organizations is one of his primary research interests.

DOI: 10.1057/9781137427519.0003

Larsåke Larsson is Senior Professor in Media & Communication Science at Örebro University, Sweden (PhD, Gothenburg University). His research fields are PR, crisis communication and journalism (journalist–politician relations). He has written and edited several Swedish university text books on PR and crisis communication.

Jacquie L'Etang is Professor of Public Relations and Applied Communication at Queen Margaret University, Scotland. She has a BA in American & English History (UEA), an MA in Commonwealth History (London) and focused her PhD on the history of the public relations occupation in the British Isles (2001). She has presented conference papers and published articles on history and historiography since 1995. She has also published on critical perspectives in public relations since 1989.

Elina Melgin, PhD, worked for Nokia Corporate Communications and the University of Art and Design before becoming CEO of ProCom, the Finnish Association of Communications Professionals. An editor and blogger for 30 years, Elina is a co-author of the acclaimed history of public relations in Finland. Her principal research interests are national identity communications and branding.

Toni Muzi Falconi is an Italian public relations professional, educator and scholar. He is senior counsel of Methodos (www.methodos.com), Professor of Public Relations at LUMSA in Rome and author of many titles. Muzi Falconi lives a peripatetic life between Italy and New York.

Natalia Rodríguez-Salcedo earned a double degree in Journalism and in Advertising and Public Relations. She received her PhD in Public Communication at the University of Navarra. Today she lectures on the History of PR and Theory of PR at the School of Communication, University of Navarra (Spain).

Betteke van Ruler is Professor emeritus in Communication Science and Corporate Communication at the University of Amsterdam. Van Ruler was Chair of the Department of Communication Science of the University of Amsterdam; she is former President of European EUPRERA and former Chair of the Public Relations Division of the ICA. She has published numerous books and articles. Her most recent title is *Reflective Communication Scrum*, an agile planning method.

DOI: 10.1057/9781137427519.0003

Astrid Spatzier, PhD (Communication Science), is a post-doctoral researcher at the University of Salzburg, Department of Communication, Public Relations and Corporate Communication Division. She is author of numerous academic publications, including books. Her main research subjects are the habitus of public relations, historiographical research, from theory into practice and health communication.

Anastasios Theofilou is Senior Lecturer in Public Relations at Bournemouth University. He holds a PhD from Athens University of Economics and Business (AUEB). His research interests focus on sponsorship, PR, crisis management and corporate social responsibility. Anastasios has been Deputy Chair of International History of Public Relations Conference (IHPRC) since 2012.

Fabio Ventoruzzo is an Italian 'public relations native'. Partner in FB&Associati, (www.fbassociati.it), he is a senior lobbying and advocacy professional. He is Director of the Studies Center of FERPI (Italian Federation of Public Relations) and teaches on the Master's in Public Affairs programme of the IlSole24Ore Business School in Rome.

Jordi Xifra is Professor at Pompeu Fabra University (Barcelona). His research focuses on the history of PR, critical PR, public affairs and public diplomacy, and his articles have been accepted for the main journals in the field. He is the co-editor of *Public Relations Inquiry*.

DOI: 10.1057/9781137427519.0003

Introduction

Tom Watson

Watson, Tom (ed.). *Western European Perspectives on the Development of Public Relations: Other Voices*. Basingstoke: Palgrave Macmillan, 2015. DOI: 10.1057/9781137427519.0004.

▶

Western European Perspectives on the Development of Public Relations: Other Voices is the fifth volume in this series of six books on national histories of public relations (PR). The 13 nations that comprise the ten chapters range from Finland and Scandinavia in the north to Greece, Italy, France and Spain on the Mediterranean rim. In two chapters – Netherlands and Belgium (Chapter 7), and Scandinavia (Sweden, Norway and Denmark; Chapter 8) – regional groupings were created for linguistic and historical reasons.

In the western half of Europe, defined by either Cold War borders or a westward-looking national aspect, with numerous languages, past histories of empire and national formation and religious and philosophical diversity, there are multiple histories of public relations. In the case of linguistically divided Belgium, there are two parallel histories from French and Dutch linguistic aspects.

As several chapters reveal, there was a strong post-war influence on the formation of agency PR from the United States, which started during the Marshall Plan era of the late 1940s and expanded later by the agency groups, primarily Burson-Marsteller and Hill & Knowlton. However, the history of PR is Germany shows strong corporate and governmental influences from the early 19th century onwards. In the Netherlands, its philosophical *voorlichting* approach to diffusion of information arises earlier from the Enlightenment.

In Austria, Belgium, France, Greece, Italy and Spain, PR was primarily a post-World War II development. For Belgium and France, like the UK, the impetus often came from wartime communicators. In Greece, ravaged by Nazi occupation, PR arose from opportunities that became evident in advertising agencies which were servicing US and UK clients. In Italy, there were pre-war examples of PR practices but the influence post-war of the United States Information Service (USIS) aided its formation as a defined sector. Italy and Greece were zones of conflict between strong Communist parties and trade unions with government, churches and business. PR was seen, at these times, as part of a democratic bulwark against Communism. Spain, nominally neutral during World War II, had delayed development of a PR sector because of exclusion of post-war aid and was further held back by Francoism until the mid-1970s. Because of these negative factors, it is the only nation where a single individual, Joaquin Maestre, can be said to have created foundations of a national PR sector and brought it into contact with international influences.

DOI: 10.1057/9781137427519.0004

In Finland, the beginnings of PR as an identified practice are linked to wartime propaganda in its conflict with Russia, while the Scandinavian nations also had mainly post-war development from government and private sector. The UK, which tracks PR to the early 20th century, developed a governmental culture of communication before World War II. Unlike other nations, its desire to form a professional PR culture came from governmental communicators and was fostered by a trade union.

Although the US model of PR agency practice can be detected now in most countries, it is notable that some sought to resist it. France from the 1950s to 1980s countered what was seen as propagandist practices with an ethical and social approach which could also be found in other countries (Belgium, The Netherlands, Greece and Scandinavia). The UK had a typically pragmatic approach while German PR was resilient, as it had existed since the late 19th century in the form of corporate communications.

Periodization has been applied in several chapters as a route to identify themes and influences with periods ranging from three in Austria, focused on post-war PR, to seven in Germany where the analysis goes back to pre-history or proto-PR influences. Overall, Western European PR has developed from a multitude of influences to create distinctive national models. Apart from imported patterns of agency operations, those national forms and structures have not been reduced to a common form of 'Euro-PR'.

DOI: 10.1057/9781137427519.0004

1

Austria

Astrid Spatzier

Abstract: *The development of public relations (PR) in Austria since 1945, across three phases, is reported and analyzed in this chapter. The first phase outlines key dates and the development of PR practice during the period of the 'Occupying Powers' from 1945 to 1955; the second refers to the period of the 'economic miracle' after 1955; and the third highlights the period from 1983 to the present, in which PR slowly became apparent in the field of communication science and practice in Austria.*

Keywords: Austria; interaction modalities; occupation-related patterns; parameters to public relations practice; public relations as a journalism function; public relations as a promotion tool

Watson, Tom (ed.). *Western European Perspectives on the Development of Public Relations: Other Voices.* Basingstoke: Palgrave Macmillan, 2015. DOI: 10.1057/9781137427519.0005.

This chapter demonstrates the development of public relations (PR) practice in Austria as an occupational field. Although there were various kinds of proto-PR practices in former times, for instance at the time of the Babenberger and Habsburger emperors, Nessmann (2004, 2008) has stated that the development of PR as an occupation in Austria began after World War II.

According to Beck, Brater and Daheim (1980), specific occupation-related patterns and procedures are required to define an occupation. Against this background and for the purpose of emphasizing the development of the occupational field, this study addresses specific occupation-related patterns and procedures in the context of public communication with an organizational frame after 1945. As a result, the orientation, tasks and interaction modalities based on the background given by witnesses lead to the understanding of PR in a timeline from 1945 onwards. Archival research is adopted to focus the facts vis-à-vis general economic, political and social history as well as in the direction of communication from the inside-out perspective. This allows the reconstruction of facts that influenced the development of PR in Austria. The results allow the drawing of conclusions regarding the characterization of occupation-related patterns and find answers to questions such as: Which types of orientation, main tasks and interactions can be identified in Austrian PR practice since 1945, and which stages can be mentioned?

First, it should be noted that orientation patterns can be seen in relation to external and internal factors. On one hand, political, economic, cultural and social circumstances and media development influenced public communication in the context of organizations. On the other, certain attitudes in society affected the economic and political minds as well as the communication. In the period of the 'Occupying Powers', for instance, the United States was mainly responsible for the awareness of public affairs. During the 'economic miracle', however, an economic boom led to an advertising boom. Crisis, conflicts and changes in the society's attitudes affected the communication after 1983.

The development of PR as an occupation in Austria

The period of Occupation

After World War II, Austria's population was characterized by human tragedies and material losses. Furthermore, a loss of orientation and

DOI: 10.1057/9781137427519.0005

identity was recognizable. Butschek (2012) claims that the first ten years after the end of World War II was the phase of reconstruction. The reconstruction, associated with the desire to overcome mistrust, assumed importance regarding the evolution of PR in Austria. Although the media was licensed under Allied supervision at that time, US Army soldiers led the promotion of public affairs, which opened up a new field for Austrian journalists. The US Army recruited Austrian journalists, photographers and individuals, who were well versed in writing, to document the good deeds of America in Austria. The Information Service Branch (ISB) and the United States Information Service (USIS) provided excellent support in fostering the development of a new democratic identity. The population had no great confidence in their leaders or their future and so were very interested in news and information. According to Petschar (2005), long queues formed in front of the newsletter outlets. Journalists and organizations were invited to report on the early economic successes and cultural events. Major construction projects, the first festival of the post-war period in Salzburg in 1945, the reopening of the State Opera and the Burgtheater in Vienna were some occasions with content for reporting. Advertising of information was undertaken by organizations with the aim to overcome mistrust and to promote the economic and infrastructural achievements in the middle of the Reconstruction era. Although the term 'public relations' was not often used, public information in the context of organizational frames was available under the terms of public affairs, press and advertising. The main tasks were similar to those of journalism and advertising. Promotional and informational texts were written in order to overcome mistrust.

According to Gröpel (1953), PR was understood as an art and therefore a special feeling was essential. Doppelreiter (1995) noted that values, such as participation and emancipation, were of particular interest in the journalistic texts of economic, political and social reorientation. The first PR course was established at the University of Vienna in the Department of Economic and Sales in 1945, and a first journal about advertising information was established a decade later in 1955 by the national advertising association. Economic scholarship was the first discipline that emphasized PR as a topic in the 1950s. Dissertations on PR written by Gröpel (1953) and Schweighardt (1954) emerged from the economic perspective at the University of Innsbruck.

DOI: 10.1057/9781137427519.0005

The economic miracle

The date of 15 May 1955 can be considered as a turning point. The signing of the State Treaty for the re-establishment of an independent, democratic Austria on that date was the formal ending of the post-war, four-power Occupation that meant freedom for Austria.

According to Brusatti (1975), the period after 1955 led to surprisingly high sales figures due to rising consumption power. The completion of large-scale infrastructure projects, such as power plants or highways, as well as cultural and sporting events of international interest, such as the Vienna Opera Ball in 1956, the FIS World Ski Championships in 1958 in Bad Gastein, the Winter Olympic Games in 1964 in Innsbruck or the winning of the Eurovision Song Contest in 1966, were indications that post-war misery has been overcome and a new national identity gained. These positive economic and socio-political events required information and application. Mainly influenced by these circumstances, advertising as a special information field expanded strongly. The first two advertising agencies were founded in Vienna in the 1950s. Brusatti (1975) emphasizes that awareness of the economic upswing led to the unfolding of economic forces and the release of extraordinary power assets. This sentiment was reflected in the advertising industry and culture. The economic success was responsible for the development of public information in the form of advertising. Thanks to the economic boom, people were quite satisfied with the national situation and did not see the necessity to ask questions or maintain critical beliefs. This was one reason why companies were not forced to explain their responsibilities regarding commercial activities. Therefore, advertising information seemed to be sufficiently effective.

The advertising boom affected PR. According to Sturmer (2014), the first two PR agencies were founded in Vienna in 1964. Ernst Haupt-Stummer (1933–) founded 'Pubrel Public Relations' and Herbert Mittag (1919–2001) the agency 'Publico'. Haupt-Stummer (2013) noted that PR's foundation in Austria emerged from the proposition to get organizational information into the media without having to pay for advertising (E. Haupt-Stummer, personal correspondence, 13 December 2013). For Haupt-Stummer, one of the Pubrel agency's first tasks was to improve the image of a production company. The company was struggling with a poor image due to the use of unhealthy substances. A report on the restoration of historic buildings using its products was placed in the media without paying for it. Nevertheless, this was an exception at that time (ibid.).

DOI: 10.1057/9781137427519.0005

PR activities were perceived as being adjacent to journalism. According to Krejci (H. Krejci, personal communication, 25 April 2013), the early regular meetings with the press were organized by journalists. The club of economic journalists invited a business representative for a talk with them every week. Another kind of PR activity indicated the proximity to journalism and advertising during the economic boom. Skoff remembered that PR practitioners went to journalists with products under their arms in order to convince them to write about these products (R. Skoff, personal correspondence, 10 June 2013).

Dohle (2012) has commented that cultural, educational, ecological, structural and economic policy milestones, such as the new Salzburger Festspiele building in 1960, the reopening of the University in Salzburg in 1962, the founding of the national park in 1971, were occasions in which the dissemination of information was undertaken through advertising in the 1960s and at the beginning of the 1970s. The increasing number of such circumstances for which information distribution seemed to be important required the coordination of presswork. Nessmann (2008) has said that a working group for press officers was founded in 1968 with the task of coordinating press conferences. However, the main PR activities were journalism-based and limited to the selection of data and the writing and dissemination of information. PR practice was thus in the form of basic media relations and recognized by political organizations and very large corporations in the form of this press-related work. Tasks were either to make positive headlines or ward off unsolicited journalistic enquiries. PR practitioners and press officers were not in management positions and normally were not invited to meetings of senior management or the executive board. Small- and medium-sized companies regarded public information as unimportant.

During the mid-1970s, an east–west divide was recognizable in Austrian PR. While a small agency scene was visible in the east (in Vienna) and resulted in the main players joining the public relations club of Austria (PRCA) in 1975, PR continued to be an unknown existence in the west. This might be due to the fact that the political and economic centre of Austria was located in the east (in Vienna). The players in the east recognized earlier the possibilities given by PR compared with the organizations in the west.

Despite the international crises, such as the oil crisis in the early 1970s, Austria's population was still satisfied. According to Urbas (1980), the people in Austria showed the highest confidence values in their

DOI: 10.1057/9781137427519.0005

government in 1974/1975 in comparison with other nations. For instance, 42 per cent of the population in Austria were very satisfied with the political actors in the government. In comparison, the highest confidence value in the United States was 16 per cent, and in Great Britain 24 per cent. Therefore, organizations were not forced to explain backgrounds or philosophies. In contrast, advertising information was considered to be sufficiently effective in this period and was still dominating the public communication in an organizational frame.

PRCA became a federation in 1980 when the 'Public Relations Verband Austria' (PRVA) was established. Its aim was to represent the interests of PR actors, increase awareness of PR and separate it from advertising. However, public relations came slowly into awareness. Dennis Buckle (1982), President of the International Public Relations Association (IPRA), stated that it was impossible that PR did not exist in Austria, but could be compared with a submarine that exists but operates out of sight. PRVA became more professional in its operations and continuously fostered the recognition of PR. The topic of recognition was in the limelight of its first national PR day in 1981, which was organized with the aim of distinguishing PR from advertising. According to Bogner (1981), this event put PR on the media agenda for the first time ever. However, society was still ignorant of it. Bogner and Hugelmann (1981) commented that the outside perspective still associated PR with journalism and advertising. It was seen as a form of promotion. Although the PRVA made extensive communication efforts in the media to increase the recognition of PR's roles and benefits in order to distinguish it from other communication disciplines, it unconsciously became closer to journalism and advertising. First, according to *PR-Szene* (1982a, p. 7), the PRVA proposed to the Association of Journalists that PR professionals be titled as 'company journalists'. Second, according to *PR-Szene* (1982b, p. 4), PRVA's intention that paid advertising in the media be clearly identified led to closer cooperation with the 'brand association', which promoted advertising of brands. Neither action improved PR's professional standing in Austria as a communication discipline.

At the beginning of the 1980s two more indications for understanding PR alongside journalism and advertising were recognizable. The trade union of journalists (1980), which published an occupational profile regarding PR, highlighted the spokesman as kind of journalist with the aim to distribute information of organizations. For this reason, press releases and advertisements were understood as PR instruments.

DOI: 10.1057/9781137427519.0005

According to the trade union, the spokesman was not characterized by a specific education or training, but he was responsible for information seeking and information distribution. The tasks were defined as follows: collecting, creating and disseminating information to general or specific publics by using media or press agencies. Above all, political and trade associations and very large companies were involved to set up such media work. Second, in 1980, the first journal that reported on PR was established; it was entitled *Bestseller*. Though it mainly focused on advertising and marketing, it also published communication topics.

In contrast to the union's positioning of PR in relation to journalism, PRVA (1984) tried to highlight a converse occupational profile that emphasized the responsibility of practitioners for the whole communication of organizations. Nevertheless, practitioners mainly followed the journalism orientation. Additionally, an article in *Bestseller* (1982) reported that PR was understood as inexpensive advertising.

Public relations in times of crisis and conflicts

Crisis, conflicts and changes in the society's attitude influenced the communication behaviour in the 1980s. Wachta (1984) considered the management of pollution crises to be the motor of development for PR. Austrians started to ask questions and express critical attitudes, which forced companies to explain their products, services and philosophy. PR was a convenient tool for this task, but it still highlighted the information paradigm. Conflict resolution was also based on that simple scheme. In this context, PR came more and more into the awareness of companies, society and communication science. The journalism orientation, however, continued to be the main model of practice emphasizing the use of journalistic skills and knowledge and associated craft skills, such as writing. PR came slowly into the awareness of communication science scholarship and education. According to Enichlmayr (1984), a traineeship in PR was introduced at the Institute for Communication Science at the University Salzburg in autumn 1982. In the winter term 1983–1984, a first PR course was established at the University of Salzburg and 'Public Relations Practice in Austria', edited by Signitzer (1984) emerged from it. This was the first observation of the status quo and dissemination of normative perspectives. Practitioners wrote about their individual recognition and understanding of PR in this edition. For instance, there were contributions from Grünzweig (1984) on PR in a commercial operation based on the example of the Eskimo-Iglo company; Kraus

DOI: 10.1057/9781137427519.0005

(1984) on PR for tourism; Summer (1984) on PR in nationalized industries using the example of the steel manufacturer Voestalpine AG in Linz; and Leitenberger (1984) about PR in the Catholic Church, to name a few examples. Due to this, the introduction of PR as a degree-level study at the University of Salzburg was led by Benno Signitzer in 1984. Moreover, the 'research group media and communication' (1984) was founded by Salzburg's Department of Communication Science with the aim of establishing scientific approaches to communication planning and consulting. According to Maier-Rabler and Renger (1986), Signitzer was appointed as the Head of the new Department of Public Relations and Organizational Communication at the university's communication science institute in 1986.

However, according to Signitzer (2002), PR was struggling with little academic and political prestige at that time. It was perceived by Signitzer as a 'dirty word' that was often associated with anti-pollution campaigns run by advocacy groups, such as Greenpeace and Global 2000, which increased the recognition of the roles and effectiveness of PR.

In 1984, PRVA inaugurated and presented its first state award. Besides honouring outstanding projects, the aim was to increase the awareness of PR among the public and the media. According to the presentations given by the companies in PRVA (1987), the first award-winning projects were close to journalism and promotion in style as they wrote about the good deeds of organizations with the aim of gaining trust and public attention.

However, the relationship between practice and communication science in order to develop quality in public relations was one of the main topics of the PRVA in the late 1980s. In 1986 the PRVA founded the scientific senate, which is responsible for the promotion of the relationship between practice and research to this day. Moreover, in 1987, the first PR study programme was established at the University of Vienna in cooperation with the PRVA. The aim was to offer a special education course at university level in order to certify the graduates.

In 1987, Hass published empirical research on PR, which can be seen as a milestone for the practice's visibility. Hass (1987, p. 64) noted that 39.6 per cent of the respondents were educated in journalism, 14.8 per cent in promotion and marketing, 13.7 per cent in trades and only 9.9 per cent gained a practice education in agencies. This result showed the continued proximity of PR to journalism. However, according to Dorer (1991), PR was a growing field. The crisis-ridden times in the 1980s and

DOI: 10.1057/9781137427519.0005

1990s led to reorientation in the direction of target groups and companies started to regard employees as an informed group.

In these decades companies also demonstrated their responsibility for conservation of the natural environment. Besides other projects, the first environmental reports were published. However, PR practitioners were still looking for situations and information which were interesting enough to be media topics. Sponsorships and celebrations were occasions in which PR was proven to be an information medium. However, the professional advertising association also recognized the importance of PR. Due to this, the association of advertising (1987) published a brochure to promote the growing field of PR. In 1991, *Horizont* was established as a journal that focused on advertising, marketing, communication and media. Using this promotional and marketing frame, PR was addressed as a topic.

With the quantitative increase of PR activities, quality came into the focus of PRVA. According to PRVA (1994), the section for agencies (APRVA) was founded in 1991 by members in order to promote quality of practice. In addition, PRVA was engaged in the linkage between theory and practice. As a result, PRVA has honoured theses from graduates since 1993 and the connection between communication science and practice was a topic of the communication departments at the Universities of Vienna and Salzburg. Arising from this crisis-ridden period, Burkart and Probst (1991) published their consensus-oriented approach which sought to build mutual trust between participants in conflict situations. In 1991, Dorer and Lojka wrote about public relations in theory and practice, and Dorer (1995) published an occupational study on political PR in Austria. Dorer (1995, p. 118) noted that press releases (83 per cent) and press conferences (66 per cent) were still seen as fundamental PR instruments.

The attractiveness of PR together with the limited academic research up to that time in Austria led to an increase in graduate theses and publications. In addition to theoretical and practical aspects, job-related problems, such as professionalization and feminization, were an issue.

Respecting the growing field, PRVA introduced another award in 1995 – the communicator of the year. Since then, practitioners with excellent communication performances have been honoured. This award is not only for PR practitioners but also for journalists and other individuals from the field of communication.

Beginning with the turn of the millennium, the interest of the PRVA to research practice increased. For this purpose, small career studies

DOI: 10.1057/9781137427519.0005

were commissioned. For instance, Depner-Berger (2003) carried out a survey on PR in companies in Salzburg. It showed that 50 per cent of the respondents used press releases as activity in the previous two years, 27 per cent emphasized events and 10 per cent advertisements. This review highlighted that media relations was still very significant.

However, the digital age has not yet led to significant changes in the mind of practitioners. According to Spatzier and Moisl (2013), the information dissemination paradigm still dominates social media interaction in Austria. Moreover, the information distribution can be seen in the context of advertising strategies. Press releases are published as part of paid media cooperation that also involves the placement of advertisements.

Conclusion

PR in Austria has moved from information to information. The main PR task is still the dissemination of information. In addition, the orientation patterns show proximity to journalism and advertising in the 60-year timeline. The occupation-related patterns in terms of orientation, tasks and interaction modalities could be seen as related to journalism and advertising during all periods and form the main paradigm. The core activity is information distribution and the main interaction modality could be seen next to the information paradigm. Although the information distribution differentiated, both the orientation and the activities remained unchanged.

The level of recognition of PR demonstrates that it has always been understood as an advertising tool and a journalism function during the Occupation period and during the 'economic miracle'. PR was not understood as a separate discipline in general and not of high importance during that time – on the contrary, it continued to be an unknown existence. Public affairs, presswork and advertising were the dominant terms and paradigms. The journalism orientation was very evident, not only in terms of skills, but also related to the association of journalism. Furthermore, the advertising orientation was central. The interaction modality was adjacent to promotion. The contextualization of PR as advertising was another indication of the advertising paradigm.

The first engagements from the inside-perspective regarding the occupational field were visible between 1975 and 1980, but still limited to the east

DOI: 10.1057/9781137427519.0005

of Austria and not recognized by the outside perspective. Although the first PR agencies were founded in the 1960s, the foundation of the PR club as an Occupation period association represented the first, limited recognition. Changes in societal attitudes and the crises-ridden periods influenced the communication since 1983. PR came more and more into the awareness of organizations in order to explain backgrounds. It was now seen as a convenient tool for providing information. However, the advertising and journalism aspects were still present. Due to this, PR was perceived as a specific information tool, which still highlights the connection to journalism and advertising. Moreover, information distribution was now not only used for external communication but also for internal target groups. Furthermore, the engagement of the PRVA since 1980 promoted the visibility of PR within the communication community. In summary, the results demonstrate that the development of PR practice in Austria is especially noticeable in quantity, and PR is still next to journalism and advertising and not a distinct discipline, profession or practice.

References

Beck, U., Brater, M. and Daheim, H. (1980) *Soziologie der Arbeit und der Berufe. Grundlagen, Problemfelder, Forschungsergebnisse* [Sociology of Work and Occupations. Basics, Problems and Research Results] (Reinbek bei Hamburg: Rowohlt).

Bestseller (1982) 'Abgrenzungsversuche zwischen PR und Corporate Identity. Versöhnungstag' [Demarcation between PR and Corporate Identity. Atonement], *Bestseller*, 26 Oktober.

Bogner, F. (1981) 'Mitgliederinformation vom 3. Dezember 1981' [Members Information from 3 December 1981], *PR-Szene* 1(1).

Bogner, F. and Hugelmann, W.-D. (1981) 'PR in der Öffentlichkeit' [PR in the Public], *PR-Szene* 1(19).

Brusatti, A. (1975) 'Wirtschaft' [Economy], in E. Weinzierl and K. Skalnik (eds) *Das neue Österreich. Geschichte der Zweiten Republik* [The New Austria. History of the Second Republic] (Graz: Styria).

Buckle, D. (1982) 'U-Boot-PR?' [PR Like a Submarine?], *PR-Szene* 4(9).

Burkart, R. and Probst, S. (1991) 'Verständigungsorientierte Öffentlichkeitsarbeit: eine kommunikationstheoretisch begründete Perspektive' [Consensus-Oriented Approach: A Communication-Theory-Based Perspective], *Publizistik*, 36(1), 56–75.

DOI: 10.1057/9781137427519.0005

Butschek, F. (2012) *Österreichische Wirtschaftsgeschichte. Von der Antike bis zur Gegenwart* [Austrian Economic History. From Antiquity to the Present] (Wien: Böhlau).

Depner-Berger, E. (2003) *Grundlagenerhebung bei PR-treibenden Unternehmen in Salzburg. Ergebnisbericht* [Baseline Survey on PR-driven Companies in Salzburg. Result Report] (Salzburg: Institut für Grundlagenforschung).

Dohle, O. (2012) 'Salzburg seit 1945 – Versuch einer „Periodisierung' [Salzburg since 1945 – Attempt at Periodization], in K. Gföllner (ed.) *Weichenstellungen im Land Salzburg. Enquete des Landtages am 9. Oktober 2012* [Decisions in Salzburg. Report of the State Parliament on 9 October 2012] (Salzburg: Landes-Medienzentrum), 3–26.

Doppelreiter, M. (1995) *Orientierung zwischen Schutt und Asche. Strategische Kommunikation in den österreichischen Jugendzeitschriften der unmittelbaren Nachkriegszeit* [Orientation between Ash and Rubble. Strategic Communication in the Austrian Youth Magazines of the Immediate Post-war Period] (Wien: Universitäts-Verlagsbuchhandel).

Dorer, J. (1991) 'Einleitung' [Introduction], in J. Dorer and K. Lojka (eds) *Öffentlichkeitsarbeit. Theoretische Ansätze, empirische Befunde und Berufspraxis der Public Relations* [Public Relations. Theory, Empirical Studies and Practice] (Wien: Braumüller)

Dorer, J. (1995) *Politische Öffentlichkeitsarbeit in Österreich. Eine empirische Untersuchung zur Public Relations politischer Institutionen* [Political Public Relations in Austria. Analysing the Public Relations of Political Institutions] (Wien: Braumüller).

Dorer, J. and Lojka K. (1991) *Öffentlichkeitsarbeit. Theoretische Ansätze, empirische Befunde und Berufspraxis der Public Relations* [Public Relations. Theory, Empirical Studies and Practice] (Wien: Braumüller).

Enichlmayr, Ch. (1984) 'Praktikum: Öffentlichkeitsarbeit – Anwendungsfeld Universität' [Practice: Public Relations – Application Field University], *Tätigkeitsbericht 1982/83/84. Informationen aus dem Salzburger Institut für Publizistik und Kommunikationswissenschaft* [Annual Report 1982/83/84. Information from the Salzburg Institute of Journalism and Communication Studies], 13, 27–29.

Gröpel, H. (1953) 'Public Relations – Eine betriebswirtschaftliche Studie' [Public Relations – An Economic Study], Dissertation (University of Innsbruck, Austria).

DOI: 10.1057/9781137427519.0005

Grünzweig, R. (1984) 'PR in einem Handelsbetrieb (Beispiel: Eskimo-Iglo)' [PR in a Commercial Establishment (Example: Eskimo-Iglo)], in B. Signitzer (ed.) *Public Relations. Praxis in Österreich* [Public Relations. Practice in Austria] (Wien: Orac).

Hass, M. (1987) *Public relations. Berufsrealität en Österreich* [Public relations: The realities of the profession in Austria (Vienna: Orac Verlag).

Kraus, W. (1984) 'Öffentlichkeitsarbeit für den Fremdenverkehr' (Beispiel: Wien) [Public Relations for the Tourism (Example: Vienna)], in B. Signitzer (ed.) *Public Relations. Praxis in Österreich* [Public Relations. Practice in Austria] (Wien: Orac), 67–78.

Leitenberger, E. (1984) 'Öffentlichkeitsarbeit der Katholischen Kirche' [Public Relations of the Catholic Church], in B. Signitzer (ed.) *Public Relations. Praxis in Österreich* [Public Relations. Practice in Austria] (Wien: Orac).

Maier-Rabler, U. and Renger, R. (1986) Über die Mitarbeiter [About the Staff Members], *Tätigkeitsbericht 1984–86. Informationen aus dem Salzburger Institut für Publizistik und Kommunikationswissenschaft* [Annual Report 1984–1986. Information from the Salzburg Institute of Journalism and Communication Studies], 20, 8–9.

Nessmann, K. (2004) 'Austria', in B. van Ruler and D. Vercic (eds) *Public Relations and Communication Management in Europe: A Nation-by-Nation Introduction to Public Relations Theory and Practice* (Berlin/New York: Mouton de Gruyter).

Nessmann, K. (2008) 'PR-Berufsgeschichte in Österreich' [PR Occupations History in Austria], in G. Bentele, R. Fröhlich, and P. Szyszka (eds) *Handbuch der Public Relations. Wissenschaftliche Grundlagen und berufliches Handeln* [Handbook Public Relations. Scientific Principles and Professional Conduct] (Wiesbaden: VS).

Petschar, H. (2005) *Die junge Republik. Alltagsbilder aus Österreich 1945–1955* [The Young Republic. Images from Austria 1945–1955] (Wien: Ueberreuter).

PR-Szene (1982a) 'Kommunikationsberufe im Wandel?' [Communications Professions in Transition?], *PR-Szene* 4(7).

PR-Szene (1982b) 'Zusammenarbeit mit Markenartiklern' [Collaboration with Brand Management], *PR-Szene* 4(4).

PRVA (1984) 'Berufsbild des Public Relations-Fachmannes' [Job Description of a PR Professional], in B. Signitzer (ed) *Public Relations. Praxis in Österreich* [Public Relations. Practice in Austria] (Wien: Orac).

DOI: 10.1057/9781137427519.0005

PRVA (1987) *Eingereichte Projekte zum Staatspreis für Public Relations der Jahre 1984 und 1985* [Submitted Projects for the National Public Relations Award in 1984 and 1985] (Wien: PRVA).

PRVA (1994) *Ein Wegweiser durch die PR-Landschaft. Agenturen im Public Relations Verband Austria* [A Guide to the PR Landscape. Agencies in the Public Relations Association] Brochure (Vienna: PRVA)

Research Group Media and Communication (1984) Forschungsgruppe Medien und Kommunikation [Research Group Media and Communication], *Tätigkeitsbericht 1982/83/84. Informationen aus dem Salzburger Institut für Publizistik und Kommunikationswissenschaft* [Annual Report 1982/83/84. Information from the Salzburg Institute of Journalism and Communication Studies], 13(73).

Schweighardt, K. (1954) 'Theorie und Praxis der öffentlichen Beziehungs- und Meinungspflege einer Unternehmung unter besonderer Berücksichtigung der sozialen Elemente' [Theory and Practice of Public Opinion Relationship and Maintaining a Company with Particular Emphasis on Social Elements], Dissertation (University of Innsbruck, Austria).

Signitzer, B. (1984) (ed.) *Public Relations. Praxis in Österreich* [Public Relations. Practice in Austria] (Wien: Orac).

Signitzer, B. (2002) 'Präsentationsunterlagen zur Entwicklung von Public Relations als Studienschwerpunkt an der Universität Salzburg' [Presentation about to the Development of Public Relations as Field of Study at the University of Salzburg], presented at DGPuK-Conference 'Public Relations als angewandte Wissenschaft – Nur eine Frage des Etiketts? Zur Unterscheidung der hochschulgebundenen Ausbildung von PR-Experten und Journalisten' [Public Relations as an Applied Science – Only a Question of the Label? To Distinguish between the University-Bound Training of PR Experts and Journalists], Lingen, Germany, 2002.

Spatzier, A. and Moisl, L. (2013) 'Social Media Meet Dialog? Analyzing the Communication Activities of Companies on Facebook', Paper presented on 3–5 October 2013, EUPRERA 2013 Congress, Barcelona.

Sturmer, M. (2014) '50 Jahre PR-Agenturen in Österreich: Talfahrt ohne Ende?' [50 Years PR-Agencies in Austria: Descent without End?], http://www.mediengeschichte.com/50-jahre-pr-agenturen-in-oesterreich-talfahrt-ohne-ende, date accessed 10 October 2014.

DOI: 10.1057/9781137427519.0005

Summer, F. (1984) 'Öffentlichkeitsarbeit in der verstaatlichten Industrie' (Beispiel: VOEST-ALPINE AG) [Public Relations in the Nationalized Industries (Example: VOEST-ALPINE AG)], in B. Signitzer (ed.) *Public Relations. Praxis in Österreich* [Public Relations. Practice in Austria] (Wien: Orac).

Trade Union of Journalists (1980) 'Berufsbild: Der Medienreferent. Referent fürÖffentlichkeitsarbeit; früher: Pressereferent' [Job Description: The Media Speaker. The Media Consultant], *Information und Meinung*, 11(2), 25–28.

Urbas, E. (1980) 'Legitimatorische Aspekte: Protestverhalten und Systemunterstützung' [Legitimating Aspects: Protest Behaviour and System Support], in L. Rosenmayr (ed.) *Politische Beteiligung und Wertewandel in Österreich* [Political Participation and Value Changes in Austria] (München/Wien: Oldenbourg).

Wachta, H. (1984) 'PR in Industriebetrieben' [Industrial PR], in B. Signitzer (ed.) *Public Relations. Praxis in Österreich* [Public Relations. Practice in Austria] (Wien: Orac).

DOI: 10.1057/9781137427519.0005

2

Finland

Elina Melgin

Abstract: *This chapter illustrates when and how the public relations (PR) profession started to develop in Finland and why certain terminology came to be used. It shows that the Finnish Association of Public Relations, founded in 1947, is one of the oldest peacetime associations of its kind in Europe. The profession had emerged almost a decade earlier, just before the outbreak of World War II. The chapter sheds light on the PR pioneers who stood out during this period in Finland's history, as well as the issues they represented.*

Keywords: Cold War; Continuation War; Finland; Finlandia News Bureau; Germany; information; Information Men; national image; propaganda; Propaganda Union; Soviet Union; Winter War

Watson, Tom (ed.). *Western European Perspectives on the Development of Public Relations: Other Voices.* Basingstoke: Palgrave Macmillan, 2015. DOI: 10.1057/9781137427519.0006.

The emergence of public relations (PR) and communications as a profession in Finland can be traced back to the Russo-Finnish wars of 1939–1940. Prior to World War II, the terms 'information' and 'propaganda' were used interchangeably in Finland without any particularly negative connotations. The use of propaganda as a new 'weapon' (Latvala, 1938) started to spread extensively during the 1930s, but the real impetus was provided by the outbreak of war in 1939. Pioneers of propaganda felt that their most important task was to safeguard Finland's national image abroad, a task that continued well beyond the end of the World War II and into the Cold War era.

Propaganda was in evidence as far back as the World's Fairs in the late 19th century, where it was used to create an image of Finland as a nation even though the country was still a part of Imperial Russia (Smeds, 1996). After the declaration of independence in 1917, the Finnish White Guard, a voluntary militia, made some attempts to create internal propaganda, but it did not yet constitute a real profession. Olavi Laine, a Finnish PR pioneer, has attempted to prove that the Mäntsälä Rebellion, a failed coup to overthrow the government in 1932, was an example of organized propaganda (Melgin and Nurmilaakso, 2012), but the creation of the first communicators' association, the Propaganda Union in 1937, is generally regarded as the starting point of the profession. The concepts of propaganda and information were used concurrently in the 1930s, each with a positive intent (Pilke, 2011; Melgin, 2014). Helsinki was awarded the Olympics in 1940 and the original purpose of the Propaganda Union was to promote the Games, but the onset of the Winter War against the Soviet Union in late 1939 brought about an abrupt change and the cancellation of the Games. The nascent association became firmly integrated into the domestic and international propaganda efforts directed by the military and the government (Melgin, 2014).

Early influences

Pan-European trends were at work in the creation of the national Propaganda Union. Walter Lippmann and Harold D. Lasswell, among others, wrote about this modern 'weaponry' in the 1920s and in less than a decade propaganda books began to appear in Finnish. One of the first publications, *National Defence and the Press*, was written in 1935 by Colonel Lasse Leander from the military forces information and press

DOI: 10.1057/9781137427519.0006

centre (Leander, 1935). Leander, like other early military propagandists, looked to Germany for training, a country with which Finland had forged close cultural and political ties since independence (Hiedanniemi, 1980; Jokisipilä and Könönen, 2013). Leander also trained the first propaganda professionals by enlisting suitable candidates, such as advertisers, writers and photographers, for military refresher courses. Among them were authors of educational books on propaganda in Finnish, and the founding members of the Propaganda Union. W. K. Latvala's *Advertising, Propaganda* (1938) emphasized propaganda as the mightiest weapon of peace and war, while Jaakko Leppo's *Propaganda, the Decisive Weapon* (1939) coached readers in propaganda work related to national defence.

According to the rules of the Propaganda Union, 'upholding and developing the willingness to defend the homeland' was defined as its main task. In order to fulfil this purpose, the Union published books and arranged presentations, also making use of material intended to publicize the Olympics, such as modest black-and-white news pamphlets produced by the Finlandia News Bureau, owned by the Union. The press was granted the right to use its material turning it, to all intents and purposes, into newspaper press releases. The rules of the News Bureau stated that it would act as an office for the Union, a move which concealed the real name from the general public. The aim of the News Bureau was to 'distribute news favourable to Finland, correct false information abroad and prevent propaganda that would be damaging to Finland' (Melgin, 2014, p. 40). The Bureau's managing director was its editor-in-chief, Jaakko Leppo. As its work was closely linked to the armed forces and the Ministry for Foreign Affairs, the two state institutions were able to oversee its work. Both the Ministry and the head of the armed forces were granted the right to appoint a representative to the Board of the News Bureau. In this way, the private Union was transformed into a state organ.

Latvala served as the Chairman of the Board of the News Bureau between 1938 and 1940. He began his career by creating an advertisement for Ford cars in Finland, establishing his own advertising agency in the 1920s, and going on to make Erva-Latvala one of the largest agencies in Finland in the 1930s. Latvala was a self-taught man who succeeded in disseminating information gleaned from the United States about the hitherto unknown profession of 'marketing', although the term was not in use in Finland at that time. 'Advertising' (*mainonta* in Finnish, or *reklam*, the more commonly used Swedish term) was the catch-all expression used to describe a field which also embraced the notion of propaganda. Latvala combined propaganda with another concept used in the United States in the 1920s, public relations. There was as yet no Finnish equivalent of the term and the literal translation, *suhdetoiminta*, was not adopted until the 1950s. Latvala participated in state propaganda during both wars, but fled the country after World War II, never to return. He provided funds for the News Bureau until the state became its main sponsor in 1940 (Melgin, 2014).

The Union was originally a private association, but it was entrusted with tasks related to national defence during the war. Other associations, such as the Finland Association in the United States, were also given propaganda-related assignments when the Winter War broke out in Finland in 1939. The Union and its News Bureau financed visits to Finland by foreign journalists. Although the Bureau's main task was to produce material for the media, an internal memorandum defined foreign press visits as its most important function. The same memorandum noted that the News Bureau already had its own correspondents in Berlin, Stockholm and New York prior to the war (ibid.).

The News Bureau was integrated into the propaganda department at army headquarters in November 1939. Although the Bureau became a code name for the army propaganda department, it was less military in nature than the rest of the organization. According to leading propagandists, a uniform was the only symbol of military affiliation (Julkunen, 1975). In addition to Leppo and Latvala, key figures in the Union were the editor-in-chief of *Suomen Kuvalehti* magazine Ilmari Turja, radio reporter Pekka Tiilikainen, authors Mika Waltari and Olavi Paavolainen and the director of Tampere City Theatre Arvi Kivimaa, who were renowned cultural luminaries in Finland. In other words, foreign propaganda was largely conducted by outstanding representatives of the press, literature and culture.

The Propaganda Union was not alone in its efforts, as the war gave rise to similar organizations. The most significant of these was the State Information Bureau (VTK). Preparations for a propaganda unit under the government commenced in September 1939, carried out by a preparatory committee consisting of military officers as well as representatives of the Foreign Department, the Finnish News Bureau (STT) and the Finlandia News Bureau. A decree on the Information Bureau came into effect in October 1939. The aim of the propaganda work was to influence and shape public opinion both domestically and internationally,

DOI: 10.1057/9781137427519.0006

in line with government policy. The Information Bureau's remit was to gather information, publish it and ensure that issues relating to national defence and the Finnish policy of neutrality were handled properly by the press and the Finnish Broadcasting Company, as well as in theatres and cinemas.

Wartime propaganda

Propaganda concerning Finland's image played an important role in all the relevant organizations. The first director of the Information Bureau, Urho Toivola, wrote in December 1939 how public opinion in different countries was dependent on views expressed by their national press. Toivola stressed that Finns should be more appreciative of foreign journalists, as they were loyal friends. Many of them had received explicit instructions from their employers to help Finland. Toivola highlighted the importance of good relationships with such journalists: 'Finland and its struggle is ultimately only a small phase in the history of mankind', and thus our task is 'to take care of the 50–100 journalists assigned to our country in such a way that the world maintains continued goodwill towards us, and public opinion will be more forceful in its demands for swift and effective action from their respective governments to help us' (Melgin, 2014, p. 79).

Toivola understood how foreign journalists could potentially exert major influence. In his opinion, the large news bureaus (Reuters, Associated Press, United Press, Tidningen Telegrambyrå) should have been given preferential treatment. It was wrong to send 'quasi-specialists' as their guides to the military front. Although they had the necessary language skills, they lacked the relevant military knowledge. Toivola's comment reveals that professionals with both propaganda and PR skills coupled with language skills were still in the minority. He also regarded reporters who wrote 'human interest' stories as important foreign journalists, because they had an impact when it came to creating a positive image of Finland in those countries that opposed Bolshevism. In essence, the Information Bureau was focused on combating communism (Holmila, 2009). Finland served as a topical example, and articles evoked sympathy towards the country, even though press relations were not handled well during the short 1939–1940 war between Finland and the Soviet Union.

DOI: 10.1057/9781137427519.0006

Those employed by the propaganda organizations were pioneers of the new profession. Propaganda has never before been conducted on such a scale both within Finland and by Finland towards other countries. These representatives from the fields of journalism, advertising and culture were instrumental in creating the 'Winter War Wonder', an image which did not appear out of thin air (Melgin, 2014). The propagandists strove daily to turn national sentiments in favour of the war. These efforts were perhaps best exemplified in Marshal Mannerheim's Daily Orders, which unified the military forces with their carefully crafted key messages and effective distribution (Mannerheim, 1939–1944). Their impact was reinforced through repetition. Every dugout and home was equipped with a radio through which propaganda was transmitted. The content created by domestic propagandists was used as a source for both domestic and foreign newspapers and radio programmes. During the Winter War, it was highlighted that the war against the Soviet Union was being fought in defence of Western culture and freedom.

Although the orderliness that had been achieved during the Winter War dwindled subsequently, the propaganda organizations remained committed to the task and produced results. While they understood the relevance of propaganda and were keen to learn, criticism of the way in which the work was being organized led to the creation of new propaganda machinery. In 1940, Prime Minister Risto Ryti set up a committee to reorganize the propaganda function. Its driving force was Lauri Puntila, who had worked in a strategic position in the State Information Bureau. The aim was to create a centralized propaganda organization that would also have greater power where censorship was concerned. In 1941, a State Propaganda Decree was issued, based on the committee's report. The new organization was called the State Information Office (VTL) and the centralized operation led to an increase in both personnel and censorship. Fresh blood had been sought, but the organization was largely populated with propagandists who had honed their craft during the Winter War. Heikki Reenpää, managing director of the Otava publishing company, was appointed director of VTL.

Continuation War

VTL and the military propaganda organization morphed into a formidable entity, but only temporarily, as further changes and staff reductions were soon required in order to cut costs. During the Continuation War (1941–1944), other propaganda organizations also underwent changes. The renaming of organizations and changes in key personnel reflected the way in which propaganda was adapted in line with fluctuations in the fortunes of war. For example, the activities of the Propaganda Union were redirected towards the civil sector. It was no longer a 'comrades-in-arms' association but rather 'a union of persons active in various fields of propaganda' (Melgin, 2014, p. 95). During the Continuation War, the Union had some 200 members, and one of its most important tasks was arranging entertainment for Finnish troops at the front.

The Continuation War did not manage to achieve the same kind of propaganda success in the foreign media that it enjoyed during the Winter War. General sympathy, if it existed outside co-warring partners Germany and Italy, was still connected with the Finnish fight against Bolshevism. In addition to seeking foreign humanitarian aid and sympathy, the propagandists strove to influence domestic sentiments in order to maintain a unified pro-war popular front. Attempts were made to evoke the Winter War spirit and provide solace for the populace through entertainment and religion, but the protracted fighting, and in particular the uncertainty that characterized the final months of the war, served to make the propaganda counterproductive. Public criticism of official propaganda increased, and the centralized propaganda system was even denounced by members of parliament (Melgin, 2014). The discussion about the dissemination of information and propaganda was, in essence, a debate about party politics and power.

Although the concept of information became dominant during the Continuation War, paradoxically censorship was tightened. The end of the war in 1944 heralded a period during which people's perceptions of the concepts of propaganda and information and their general understanding of the profession changed. Propaganda and censorship became associated in the general public's mind with a war that had been lost and with poor foreign policy choices. In light of this, propagandists wanted to drop the term 'propaganda', albeit with little success, as the word had become entrenched in the language, and in practice the general public was unable to tell the difference between propaganda and information. The concepts continued to be used alongside each other, especially in PR work targeted at other countries. National propaganda was also used in the neutral sense of 'creating awareness'.

DOI: 10.1057/9781137427519.0006

Propaganda had to be relegated to the past, along with the lost war. In December 1944, the State dismantled the Continuation War propaganda organization. An interim peace agreement was reached with the Soviet Union that included a clause prohibiting the dissemination of war propaganda. In turn, the State Information Office and similar war-related organizations were closed. Any propaganda directed against the Soviet Union was also prohibited. The wartime propaganda organizations were replaced with a new State Information Office, with largely curtailed duties. The dismantling of the propaganda organization in 1944 also led to a reduction in censorship. Other propaganda organizations with new names, such as the Finlandia Union, were closed down within a few years (ibid.). State information activities diminished as the censorship and propaganda offices were dismantled, and the Ministry for Foreign Affairs was given the responsibility of reshaping the national image, changing the concept from brothers-in-arms with Germany to friends of the Soviet Union.

In 1945, a State committee, headed by Minister Asko Ivalo, considered the role of the information office during peacetime. Amongst the committee members was Väinö Meltti, who had been a political prisoner during the war. The post-war years saw numerous wartime left-wing political prisoners rise to prominence, although their influence was short-lived. Information professionals realized that during peacetime, state information should be perceived as a 'mediation tool' and a 'government auxiliary' rather than as a propaganda mechanism representing the centralized wartime power machinery (Committee Report, 1945, p. 32).

The Committee Report on the reorganization of information activities drew attention to the high cost of producing bulletins and press clippings. Specialists consulted by the committee noted that, in future, active information dissemination and staff capable of communicating in foreign languages were needed at the Ministry for Foreign Affairs: '... particularly when following broadcasts from the Soviet Union, as other direct connections between our press and the Soviet Union are slow and inadequate' (ibid., p. 11). Other envisaged tasks for the new communications organization included relations with journalists, as well as dissemination of press releases. Consequently, all tasks related to foreign information reverted to the Ministry for Foreign Affairs and state information functions were divided between ministries. There were no formal regulations, although civil servants were bound by confidentiality. State communications became more passive and remained so until the 1950s.

DOI: 10.1057/9781137427519.0006

A clear change was evident in government reports of the day. During the war, propaganda and information as a concept had a clear role in such reports, but after the war, information as a profession completely disappeared from the reports (Melgin, 2014).

Reorganization after World War II

Despite the transition to peace, journalism and information were still living in extraordinary times and many national functions, such as industrial production and housing, remained under tight control. Finland's relations with the Soviet Union were a particular source of tension. The mighty neighbour had to be treated with the utmost care, in order to avoid unnecessary irritation caused by careless comments in the media. The new foreign policy, directed by President Juho Paasikivi, dictated the preconditions for the delivery and content of information.

Finland's post-war reputation was dominated by its delicate relationship with the Soviet Union. As the content of existing PR material had become obsolete (ibid.), the communications committee proposed strengthening foreign PR through new publications and documentary films. Visits to Finland for foreign journalists were still one of the main channels for international PR. Radio programmes in various languages were also highlighted in the Committee Report. The most significant proposal in the latter concerned the centralization of information activities. To this end, it was concluded that 'there are no compelling reasons for the total centralization of state information and propaganda' (Committee Report, 1945, pp. 27, 32).

The task of reorganizing and defending state propaganda was by no means cordially conducted in a period during which the nation was endeavouring to erase the war from its collective consciousness. Propaganda had already come in for heavy criticism from journalists and politicians in the latter stages of the war. Post-war, the political right–left divide culminated in arguments over the role of propaganda, although parliamentary discussion provided no alternatives as to how war propaganda and information should have been organized. It proved impossible to separate the two issues, as war propaganda had been a key tool for managing both domestic and foreign policy in Finland.

Finally, censorship's abolition required further scaling-down of the State Information Office until it was closed. Propaganda became a

DOI: 10.1057/9781137427519.0006

scapegoat and was condemned like a war criminal. The centralized Information Office came to symbolize the lost war and the poor decisions that had led to the loss. It was necessary to wipe the slate clean in order to distance itself from the war. As people could easily point fingers at propaganda and censorship, the centralized organization (not the people working for it or even the highest military command) had to bear the brunt of the blame. Lauri Puntila was cast as the grand censor, but the dust soon settled and he was able to embark on a new academic career as Professor of Political History at the University of Helsinki. Information officers returned to their civil professions in universities, press offices, ministries and art institutions. Gentlemen's agreements ensured that no one would ever speak about what had transpired during the war years (Näre and Kirves, 2008).

Although most propagandists returned to their civil professions after the war, some wanted to contribute to promoting Finland's national image in their civil roles. These men, who were referred to as 'propaganda officers' even after the war, established an informal advisory board. They called themselves the 'Information Men', serving primarily as civil servants in governmental bodies, such as the Ministry for National Relief, the Ministry of Finance and the National Broadcasting Company. The term 'communications' was rarely used to describe the profession in those days, although it inherited several concepts from the wartime propaganda era. Communications professionals in Finland still use words such as strategy, tactics or positioning.

Information Men

In December 1947, the Information Men established a public PR association called Tiedotusmiehet (literally the Information Men Association, but officially the Society of Public Relations). Finland was one of the early European nations to form such a professionally oriented body.

The Tiedotusmiehet archives are currently located in the National Archives in Helsinki, although some undated original presentations and authentic copies of wartime documents can be found in the office of the current organization, ProCom (the Finnish Association of Communications Professionals). An interesting detail is that two strategic pioneers, Jaakko Leppo and Colonel Leander, participated in the Association's work during its infancy. The Association had between 100

DOI: 10.1057/9781137427519.0006

and 200 members in its early years, of whom only a very small minority were women. The two men were united by their common war experiences, which influenced their views on effective state-level communications. In essence, Tiedotusmiehet was the direct successor to the Propaganda Union and other related wartime propaganda organizations.

Tiedotusmiehet assumed an active societal role, not least by providing comments on the Report of the National Communications Committee. The letter signed by its first chairman, Yrjö Kankaanpää, included criticism of the state of national communications and proposed improvements (Committee Report, 1945, p. 32). Alongside this committee work, another committee was established based on an initiative by Finland's Industrial Union and Central Organization for Finnish Forestry Industries to consider how to use PR to promote foreign trade. It was evident that communications as a new profession had started to arouse interest in the corporate sector as well.

The second committee promoting exports conducted research on corresponding activities in Sweden, France and the United States, and concluded that Finland was lagging behind other countries. It called for more PR material, promotional films and further co-operation to serve the export sector. The committee also proposed increasing resources for international art exhibitions. Even the Government Report of 1947 mentioned communications as a means of revitalizing the economy. It stated that national-level communications had attempted 'to encourage national industries to be more efficient and to mediate between consumers and producers' (Government Report, 1947, p. 177).

The managing director of the Union for Finnish Work and active PR association influencer, Olavi Laine, eagerly promoted PR as a new concept, distinct from propaganda and information. He belonged to a handful of Finns who used the term 'public relations' (Pietilä, 1980). Asla and Fulbright scholarships to the United States were vital in building and transferring knowledge about PR as a new concept. In addition, European PR literature and critics were studied as there was no training available in Finland at that time (Åberg, 2012, p. 29). For a surprisingly high number of Finnish politicians and researchers, US scholarships offered an escape from political pressures as late as the 1980s (Tarkka, 2012, pp. 102–104).

Improving foreign PR was a popular topic at Tiedotusmiehet during its early years. The general consensus in the new association was that insufficient information was being disseminated abroad; too much of it was based on rumour and hearsay. Several meetings were dedicated to the post-war national image, particularly between 1947 and 1959. The subject was a topical one as foreign policy was dominated by the Cold War. Articles were published in the press, and parliament discussed national PR, albeit using the word 'information' at that time. Appropriately enough, Finland's national image was the subject of the very first national PR Professionals Days, held in 1949, and annually for ten years afterwards.

References

Åberg, L. (2012) 'Ammattina viestintä' [Communications as a Profession], in P. von Hertzen, E. Melgin and L. Åberg (eds) *Vuosisata suhdetoimintaa: Yhteisöviestinnän historia Suomessa* [History of Public Relations in Finland] (Keuruu: Otava).

Committee Report (1945: 32 and attachment 1949) Valtion tiedotustoiminnan uudelleen järjestämisestä [Committee Report on the Restructuring of State Information] (Helsinki: Valtioneuvoston kirjapaino).

Government Reports (1938–1948) *Hallituksen kertomukset, Suomen valtiopäiväasiakirjat* [Reports AIV 1938–1948. Finnish Government Reports, Finland's Parliamentary Documents] (Helsinki: Valtioneuvoston kirjapaino).

Hiedanniemi, B. (1980) *Kulttuuriin verhottua politiikkaa: Kansallissosialistisen Saksa kulttuuripropaganda Suomessa 1933–1940* [Politics under the Veil of Culture: German National Socialist Culture Propaganda in Finland 1933–1940] (Helsinki: Otava).

Holmila, A. (2009) *Talvisota muiden silmin: maailman lehdistö ja Suomen taistelu* [The Winter War through the Eyes of Others: The World Press and Finland's Struggle] (Jyväskylä: Atena).

Jokisipilä, M. and Könönen, J. (2013) *Kolmannen valtakunnan vieraat: Suomi Hitlerin Saksan vaikutuspiirissä 1933–1944* [The Third Reich's Visitors: How Finland Was Influenced by Hitler's Germany 1933–1944] (Keuruu: Otava).

Julkunen, M. (1975) *Talvisodan kuva: Ulkomaiset sotakirjeenvaihtajat Suomessa v. 1939–1940* [The Winter War through Foreign War Correspondents' Eyes 1939–1940] (Turku: Turun yliopisto).

DOI: 10.1057/9781137427519.0006

Latvala, K. W. (1938) *Mainonta, propaganda* [Advertising, Propaganda] (Helsinki: Erva-Latvala).

Leander, L. (1935) *Maanpuolustus ja sanomalehdistö* [National Defence and the Press] (Helsinki: Otava).

Leppo, J. (1939) *Propaganda, ratkaiseva ase* [Propaganda, the Decisive Weapon] (Helsinki: Otava).

Mannerheim, C. G. E. (1939–1944) 'Orders of the day of the Commander-in-Chief'. Mannerheim Museum website, http://www.mannerheim-museo.fi/arkisto/ylipaallikon-paivakaskyt/, date accessed 17 August 2014.

Melgin, E. (2014) *Propagandaa vai julkisuusdiplomatiaa? Taide ja kulttuuri Suomen maakuvan viestinnässä 1937–1952* [Propaganda or Public Diplomacy? Art and Culture in Finnish National Image Communications] (Helsingin yliopisto: Unigrafia).

Melgin, E. and Nurmilaakso, M-L. (2012) 'Alan järjestäytyminen' [Unionizing the Branch], in P. von Hertzen, E. Melgin and L. Åberg (eds) *Vuosisata suhdetoimintaa: Yhteisöviestinnän historia Suomessa* [History of Public Relations in Finland] (Keuruu: Otava).

Näre, S. and Kirves, J. (2008) *Ruma sota: Talvi- ja jatkosodan vaiettu historia* [Ugly War: The Hushed-Up History of the Winter and Continuation Wars] (Johnny Kniga: Helsinki).

Pietilä, J. (1980) *Suomalaisen suhdetoiminnan kehitys* [The Development of Finnish Public Relations] (Tampere: Tampereen yliopisto).

Pilke, H. (2011) *Julkaiseminen kielletty: rintamakirjeenvaihtajat ja päämajan sensuuri 1941–1944* [Publication Forbidden: Frontline Correspondents and HQ Censorship] (Helsinki: Suomalaisen Kirjallisuuden Seura).

Smeds, K. (1996) *Helsingfors – Paris: Finlands utveckling till nation på världsutställningarna 1851–1900* [Helsinki Paris: Finland's Development into a Nation as Viewed through the World's Fairs 1851–1900] (Helsingfors: Svenska litteratursällskapet i Finland).

Tarkka, J. (2012) *Karhun kainalossa* [In the Arms of the Russian Bear] (Helsinki: Otava).

Tiedotusmiehet ry Arkisto 1947–1959 Tiedotusmiesten vuosikertomukset, johtokunnan kokoukset, lehtileikkeet [Finnish Public Relations Association's Archive, Including Annual Reports, Board Meeting Minutes, Press Clippings] (Helsinki: National Archive of Finland).

DOI: 10.1057/9781137427519.0006

3
France

Bruno Chaudet, Valérie Carayol and Alex Frame

Abstract: *This chapter deals with the development of public relations (PR) as a professional field in France, from 1945 to the late 1980s. Not initially considered as a strategic management function, French PR sought to gain legitimacy in its early years, implicitly differentiating itself from the model of North American PR by which it was inspired, through a focus on the ethical dimension of the profession and its distinction from the related professions of journalism and advertising. Professional associations reflected these concerns and played a key role in helping the profession construct its identity. Social evolutions, especially the civil unrest associated with May 1968, can also be seen to have influenced the development of PR, underlining deeper social trends and the growing need for social dialogue both within organizations and externally. Successive governments and the public sector, in general, also played an important role in legislating and then legitimizing the profession on several occasions. By the late 1980s, the strategic dimension of the PR/communications function had become accepted in many major organizations.*

Keywords: AFREP; France; PR; relations publiques

Watson, Tom (ed.). *Western European Perspectives on the Development of Public Relations: Other Voices.* Basingstoke: Palgrave Macmillan, 2015. DOI: 10.1057/9781137427519.0007.

    DOI: 10.1057/9781137427519.0007

The term 'relations publiques', as used in France, is generally associated with a relatively narrow range of communications practices, at the centre of which are press relations and events coordination. As the professional field of communication practices gradually widened and diversified, it came to be labelled as 'corporate', 'institutional', 'organizational' or 'strategic communications', rather than as 'public relations' (PR). The latter term now has a somewhat old-fashioned ring in French, reminiscent of a normative set of professional practices which were common until the 1980s, but which seem out of date today (D'Almeida and Carayol, 2014).

However, in the course of its history, the term was used extensively by the community of French communications professionals, as the profession developed, along with corresponding specialized higher education courses and research. Today virtually no French university course may be found in 'relations publiques', though would-be professionals are trained in 'organizational' or 'strategic communications', and much research has been conducted into this professional field since the 1980s.

The way the field has evolved historically has been studied in French-speaking Canada (Dumas, 2010) (Maisonneuve, 2004) and in Belgium (Gryspeerdt, 2004), much more than in France, as several scholars have pointed out (Walter, 1995) (Carayol, 2004, 2010). The growing interest for historical research over the previous ten years or so, in Europe, encourages us to examine how PR evolved in France, and to identify new sources for this.

This chapter underlines a few important aspects of the way the PR profession appeared and developed in France, but it is by no means an exhaustive approach. Rather, it seeks to raise key questions and thus pave the way for future research. It is based on interviews conducted between April and September 2014 with key figures who witnessed or played a part in the way the profession evolved, as well as archive material from the French Public Relations Association (AFREP) and both professional and scientific documents relating to the profession's history. It focuses on the way the profession gradually constructed its legitimacy, from the pioneers in the first half of the 20th century up to the 1980s, when communication became more widely recognized as a strategic function within the organization.

DOI: 10.1057/9781137427519.0007

The beginning: when public relations became relations publiques

The origins of French PR and the beginning of its development as a professional field are closely linked to the Marshall Plan at the end of World War II. The ensuing contacts between French and American businesses led many French companies to borrow and adopt American management techniques, including PR as an integrated management function.

Yet, obviously, companies had already been confronted with the question of communications prior to World War II (Malaval, 1996), long before such considerations were recognized as 'PR'. As French PR consultant Jean-Pierre Beaudoin, founder and former director of the industry body Syntec Relations Publiques, points out, Michelin was probably one of the first major organizations to develop 'PR practices' in France. The company began supplying tyres for cyclists in 1898. In 1900, it published the first *Michelin Guide* for professional drivers. In 1910, it created the first road signs displaying the names of the towns into which people were driving, and then in 1918 it produced signposts indicating directions and distances. Through this pioneering PR work, Michelin sought to identify the interests of its publics and to build relations with them by making their lives easier:

> Michelin is a company which understood, virtually from its creation that by producing communication tools useful to the people who were going to buy its tyres, it would be able to establish its brand on its territory. So they made maps, guides, signposts ... and they occupied a brand territory with communication tools. (J.-P. Beaudoin, personal communication, 26 May 2014)

Notwithstanding such early exceptions, most commentators record the beginning of the profession in France as 1947, the year when François Lulé-Dejardin (Shell, France), Lucien Matrat (Caltex) and Jean Choppin de Janvry (Esso) went to the US on a 'productivity mission', and discovered PR. 'When they returned to France, they were seen as pioneers, setting up PR departments in their respective companies' (Viale, 1997, p. 39, our translation). Following the example of the oil companies, many others sent their employees to learn American management techniques, Among the methods was what Edward Bernays (2007) termed 'engineering consent', or which Ivy Lee described less controversially as a way for companies to explain to their publics what their roles were and why they were so

DOI: 10.1057/9781137427519.0007

important for the local, regional and national communities. Public relations professionals thus sought to 'modify the public's representation of the oil industry by providing "objective" explanations to "opinion leaders"' (Viale, 1997, p. 59). Esso organized public meetings, published the magazine *Pétrole et Progrès* and produced educational materials for teachers.

The companies that imported PR into France thus adopted it in a similar spirit to that of the practices Michelin had developed: building relationships with certain categories of publics, which were not limited to clients. 'The market is seen as a part of society as a whole, and the needs of relevant publics are taken into account in their social dimension and not merely in terms of the market' (ibid., p. 59). If the oil companies were the first to develop teaching materials, comments Jean-Pierre Beaudoin, it was as a result of public opinion in France following the Suez Crisis in 1956 and the unpopularity of the American oil conglomerates who were seen to be making huge profits by exploiting oil wells situated in the Middle East:

> This reductionist vision of the Oil Industry led companies in this sector to develop educational materials to explain what petroleum was. They explained the process from initial exploration to the finished product, showing all the different professions involved, the investments, the transformations, and all the benefits of oil derivatives, including plastic. These were the first teaching materials produced by companies. (J.-P. Beaudoin, personal communication, 26 May 2014)

Though the first PR departments were to be found in private corporations, it did not take long for public-sector organizations to adopt the function too. Among these were the French railways (SNCF), whose image had deteriorated during World War II, and the 'Post and Telecommunications' Ministry, which set up a large PR service in 1952, employing between 150 and 200 people. Other Ministries also developed the function from 1958 onwards.

The quest for legitimacy

The field started to organize itself as a sector of professional activity in the 1950s or early 1960s, as the first PR agencies were set up: 'Relations' by Henri Pineau and Géo-Charles Véran, the 'Office Français des Relations Publiques' by Georges Serrel, 'Information & Entreprise' by Jacques Coup de Fréjac. In 1950, the first professional association for PR, founded by a group of pioneering figures around Jean Choppin de Janvry and Lucien Matrat, sought to develop practices and a theory of PR in France. It was named 'The Glass House Club' (Club de la maison de verre), in reference to Ivy Lee's Declaration of Principles and notably the principles of transparency and telling the whole truth. The Club translated the American term into French and named its activity 'relations publiques'. However, this translation has since been criticized as being at the root of a subsequent widespread misunderstanding, in France (though not in Belgium or French-speaking Canada, where the same term is used), of what PR means. Indeed, in French, the term is more readily understood as 'relationships which are public', and, for many, 'relations publiques' has come to be taken as events and press relations, putting very little emphasis on the strategic function of PR. Although this interpretation is itself open to discussion, it should be noted that Syntec RP, the main professional body today, recently replaced the adjective 'publiques' in its name with the noun 'publics', thus clarifying and underlining the idea of 'relationships with publics'.

Independently of such semantic considerations, practitioners in the early days worked to establish their profession's legitimacy. From early on, there was a negative image surrounding PR that Anne-Marie Cotton, Belgian PR academic and long-time member of the European Confederation of Public Relations (CERP), suggests was seen as 'a network of young men and young ladies from good families' (personal communication, 30 May 2014). Professionals worked to distinguish PR from journalism and commercial advertising, and notably from the notion of propaganda. This notion was present in early American PR, with the Creel Committee (CPI – Committee on Public Information) and the work of Edward Bernays. Some of the French PR pioneers, such as Jacques Coup de Fréjac, had worked in military information during World War II, yet sought to distance themselves from what was perceived as the US model of propaganda.

Another professional body, APROREP, was set up in 1952 by several members of the 'Glass House Club', who wanted to lay down ethical principles defining good PR practice. In 1954, they created a 'Professional Code for PR', listing certain guidelines and objectives for PR practitioners. It stated that:

> The specialisation of functions and activities imposed by technical progress has constructed barriers between the different groups making up society, and between the individuals forming these groups. The result is insufficient

DOI: 10.1057/9781137427519.0007

communication and a lack of mutual knowledge which can lead to a total breakdown of relations .... What we call Public Relations are the activities carried out by a group in order to establish and maintain good relations between the members of the group, and between the group and different sectors of public opinion. (Quoted in Walter, 1995, p. 35, our translation)

Early French PR thus incorporated a critical vision of industrialized society, along with the idea that it could solve the problems and social antagonisms associated with it. This involved developing relations with the social environment in a broad sense: 'Staff, shareholders, distributors, clients and suppliers, teachers, the press, trade unions, public administrations, legal and executive bodies, etc' (ibid.). The APROREP code was replaced in 1965 by IPRA's International Code of Ethics (Code of Athens), but this global dimension of PR was not understood immediately by business leaders, who only began to take into account the global environment and their relationships with their publics after the social conflicts a decade on in the late 1960s.

The mid-to-late 1950s were a time when many new professional bodies were created, illustrating both the desire to find a consensual definition of PR and the difficulty of doing so. The APROREP and the 'Glass House Club' joined forces in 1955 to become the AFREP ('French Association for Public Relations'). In the same year, Géo-Charles Véran founded the 'National Syndicate of PR Agents' (SNARP) while Jacques Coup de Fréjac and Georges Serel set up the 'National Syndicate of PR Consultants' (SNCRP). André Hurtrel created the 'National Union of Press Agents' (UNAP) in 1956, along with Philippe Boiry. In an interview carried out by Janine Aubouy Dutreix in 2013, Boiry explained that the UNAP recruited many members from outside the field of PR in order to survive 'both financially and in terms of numbers'.

The work of professional bodies and their desire to draw up the boundaries of a professional field and to design ethical guidelines to distinguish PR from advertising and propaganda eventually bore fruit in the form of a law. In 1964, the 'Arrêté Peyrefitte' named after the Information Minister at that time, Alain Peyrefitte, made a distinction between propaganda and PR, in its first article. Jean-Baptiste de Bellescize of Weber Shandwick and Porter Novelli and past President of Syntec RP points out (personal communication, 6 May 2014):

The Peyrefitte Law was very important since it structured the professional communications field around three incompatible functions: journalism,

DOI: 10.1057/9781137427519.0007

advertising and PR. These functions were structured in a similar way to the legal professions: it's impossible to be a defence lawyer, a prosecutor and a judge at the same time. We can't be journalists, advertisers and PR professionals at the same time.

In the second half of the 1960s, the different professional bodies started working more closely together, and eventually five major syndicates/unions came together, in 1971, to form the French Public Relations Federation (FFRP), a body which existed until 1996, and which did a lot of work to draw up and enforce a common ethical code. However, the question of boundaries between professions was still ongoing, as shown by the editorial that Jacques Coup de Fréjac wrote in the AFREP newsletter in 1972, once more making the case for distinguishing PR from commercial, financial and institutional forms of advertising:

> During PR's formative years in France, certain executives in the public or private sector, or even certain professionals made honest mistakes as to where exactly the limits between PR, advertising and journalism lay. Those who continue to do so today are dishonest and their behaviour is yet more reprehensible since they are motivated by personal interests. Between neighbouring territories, we find natural or legislative boundaries. Sometimes there are zones of no man's land. This is where bandits operate. Our profession is no place for such surreptitious behaviour. (*Nouvelles brèves de l'AFREP*, no. 76, February 1972, our translation)

PR after the 1968 social unrest

If the professional bodies played a role in helping the profession to develop internally during the 1950s and 1960s, it was not until the summer of social unrest and the General Strike in France – stemming from the student protests in 1968 – that many business leaders started to take on board the importance of communication. Indeed, although PR had long been underlining the importance of building relations with different publics, top management in the 1960s was generally not prone to dialogue, either internally or externally. In Philippe Boiry's view, 'in France, the last people to understand the role of press officers were the company directors themselves' (Aubouy Dutreix, interview, 2013).

This attitude to internal relations had been observed in 1950 during the debate surrounding the introduction of a minimum wage for workers in

DOI: 10.1057/9781137427519.0007

France, a move to which the French Employers' Council (CNPF) had always been opposed. When the State finally imposed this measure, as Henri Weber (1991) reports, the debate was particularly fierce during negotiations with the CNPF when trying to establish what a 'minimum subsistence salary' might be, as company owners argued about how few calories and how few clothes an employee needed to survive. In stark contrast to professional PR bodies' utopian discourse about employee relations, this was the period of triumphant Taylorism when internal PR had no place in the company.

Yet Taylorism was soon losing its halo and several reports over the next couple of decades underlined the importance of taking human relations into account within companies. Senior civil servant François-Bloch Lainé (1963) published an influential book encouraging employers to focus on developing relations within their companies. Similar ideas were to be found in the report 'Information in the Company', published in 1972 by the 'Young Business Leaders' Organisation' (Floris, 1996, p. 119), and again in the report entitled 'Reforming Companies' submitted to President Valéry Giscard d'Estaing in 1974 by Pierre Sudreau. As early as 1969, Jacques Baumel was made Secretary of State in Charge of PR, an office he held until 1972, under Prime Minister Chaban-Delmas, which contributed significantly to raising the profile of PR and press relations.

Indeed, after the shock of 1968, the early 1970s saw the creation of integrated 'Information–Communication' services not only in many large French companies, such as Saint-Gobain and Peugeot (1970), L'Oréal and Renault (1973), but also in the Employers' Council (CNPF) itself (1970). The latter set up a 'General Information Service' headed by Michel Frois, who had previously worked for the Armed Forces PR and Information Service (SIRPA). Henri Weber (1991) interprets the emergence of these new services as a direct result of the General Strike of 1968, in which several top managers had been taken hostage in their own factories, triggering the 'media turn' taken by business leaders. With a wider, more strategic scope, the new 'Information–Communication' services often encompassed both existing internal communication, which had been developed by human resources, and external communication, which had been the central activity of the PR department.

At its 1972 congress, held under the auspices of 'Growth, the Company, and People', the CNPF held debates in front of 175 journalists from the written press, on the themes of 'Growth and Society' and 'People in Companies'. Communication was central to these debates, which centred on the 'communication spirit' and workers who were becoming more and more qualified and who needed to be informed about what the company was doing. At this congress, Antoine Riboud, CEO of Danone, gave a talk which has come to be known as 'The Marseille Speech'. In it, he analyzed the recent evolutions in French society and called upon business leaders to set up information systems involving their staff. He urged them to look beyond the economic dimension and to embrace other aspects of the human condition, such as solidarity, responsibility, and personalization. He pleaded for companies to take on responsibilities beyond the factory walls, in society at large.

Jacques Coup de Fréjac's editorial in the December 1972 issue of the *Glass House Review*, inspired by this speech, stated that, 'the CNPF had invited us – implicitly or explicitly – to move our services in this direction. If these things happen without us, we'll be the only ones to blame. If they are to happen with us, if we are to orchestrate them, then we have no choice but to assume the "global" nature of the communication function' (*La Maison de verre* no. 80, December 1972, our translation). In this way, the global communication function was seen to supersede that of PR, making information, and hence both internal and external PR, more central to that function.

Five years later, while at the Finance Ministry, future President Valéry Giscard d'Estaing set up the 'General Service for Relations with Publics' (Delorme, 2000). This was another public-sector reform which played an important role in generalizing public relations. As Jean-Pierre Beaudoin (personal communication) remembers:

> The massive arrival of PR in the public administration was down to Giscard. When he created the General Service for Relations with Publics, this was set up in 101 local government administrations. Suddenly, it was on another scale. At that time, the profession had more people working in the public sector than in the private sector. The public sector acted as a catalyst.

Underlying trends in the public sphere

In the late 1970s and 1980s, the PR function became more widely established and accepted in France. From a sociological point of view, according to Jean-Pierre Beaudoin, this can be linked to three underlying

DOI: 10.1057/9781137427519.0007

trends. The first of these was demographic, as the school-leaving age increased and the baccalaureate became increasingly widespread:

> It was a radical change: France became intelligent. Not that it had been unintelligent previously, but increasingly people's opinions were considered legitimate, they spoke out, and the media covered what they said. This led to a public sphere in which people considered they had things to say, and in which the media published them. (ibid.)

A second, accompanying factor was the growing number and popularity of press magazines catering for people's desire to understand the economy and workplace-related issues, from *L'Expansion* (1967) to *Le Nouvel Economiste* (1976):

> When you have people reading magazines which talk about company-related issues, all of a sudden you're faced with people who not only consider themselves intelligent, but who also consider themselves informed and hence competent. (Jean-Piere Beaudoin, personal communication)

The third factor was linked to changes in the law, triggered by the Sudreau Report (1975), in employer–employee relations in the workplace. It was the first report to highlight the importance of internal communications in legitimizing the decision-making process. The Sudreau Report recommended reforming industrial relations procedures so as to involve employee representatives in the internal decision-making processes of companies.

On the political level, François Mitterrand's election in 1982 and Michel Rocard's project to incorporate project-management techniques in public-sector administrations created further need for experts in public-sector communication, alongside the growing need for experts in private-sector PR and communications strategy.

The function of Communications Director or DIRCOM (Walter, 1995) was thus born in France in the 1980s. In subsequent decades, it went on to become generalized in both public and private sectors, consolidating its strategic dimension, adapting to an ever-changing communications landscape, revolutionized by the advent of digital communications. Yet, with the benefit of hindsight, many of the questions raised today, for example by the merging of publics and content providers in the digital sphere or the concerns about fading distinctions online between the roles of journalists, advertisers and legitimate mouthpieces of the organization, can be seen to resonate with the age-old concerns which shaped the professional field of PR during its formative years in France.

DOI: 10.1057/9781137427519.0007

Note: People interviewed for this chapter (with our thanks): Jean Amyot d'Inville, Jean-Pierre Beaudoin, Annie Blin, Lionel Chouchan, Anne-Marie Cotton, Jean-Baptiste de Bellescize, Jean-François Flahault, Frédérique Pusey, and Thierry Wellhoff.

References

Bernays, E. (2007) *Propaganda, comment manipuler l'opinion en démocratie* [Propaganda: How to Manipulate Opinion in a Democracy] (Paris: Zones).

Bloch-Lainé, F. (1963) *Pour une réforme de l'entreprise* [Reforming Companies] (Paris: Seuil).

Carayol, V. (2004) 'Public Relations in France', in B. van Ruler and D. Verčič (eds) *Public Relations and Communication Management in Europe. a Nation-by-Nation Introduction to Public Relations Theory and Practice* (Berlin/New York: Mouton De Gruyter).

Carayol, V. (2010) 'PR professionals in France: An Overview of the Sector', *Journal of Communication Management*, 14(2), 167–177.

D'Almeida, N. and Carayol, V. (2014) 'La communication organisationnelle, une question de communauté' [Organizational Communication: A Question of Community], *Revue Française des Sciences de l'Information et de la Communication*, 4, http://rfsic.revues.org/870, date accessed 29 September 2014.

Delorme, G. (2000) *De Rivoli à Bercy. Souvenirs d'un inspecteur des finances 1952–1998* [From Rivoli to Bercy. Memoirs of a Treasury Official 1952–1998] (Paris: Institut de la gestion publique et du développement économique).

Dumas, M. (2010) *Les relations publiques. Une profession en devenir* [Public relations. A profession of the future] (Quebec: Presses Universitaires du Québec).

Floris, B. (1996) *La communication managériale* [Managerial Communication] (Grenoble: Presses Universitaires de Grenoble).

Gryspeerdt, A. (2004) 'Relations publiques et recherche en communication' [Public Relations and Communication Research], *Hermès*, 38, 148–154.

Maisonneuve, D. (2004) *Les relations publiques: le syndrome de la cage de Faraday* [Public Relations: The Faraday's Cage Syndrome] (Québec: Presses Universitaires du Québec).

DOI: 10.1057/9781137427519.0007

Malaval, C. (1996) 'L'histoire des entreprises à travers sa presse' [Company History through the Company Press], *Entreprises et Histoire*, 11 (March), 49–60.

Viale T. (1997) *La communication d'entreprise: pour une histoire des métiers et des écoles.* [Company Communication: A History of the Profession and Its Models] (Paris: L'Harmattan).

Walter, J. (1995) *Directeur de communication, les avatars d'un modèle professionnel* [Communication Director, the avatars of a professional model] (Paris: L'Harmattan).

Weber, H. (1991) *Le parti des patrons: Le CNPF, 1946–1990.* [The Bosses' Party: The CNPF, 1946–1990] (Paris: Seuil).

DOI: 10.1057/9781137427519.0007

4

Germany

Günter Bentele

Abstract: *Modern public relations (PR) in Germany started at the beginning of the 19th century. Before then, a time in which medieval rulers, emperors, princes, churches and poets communicated publicly and when communication instruments were used that were similar to later PR instruments, can be called the prehistory of PR. In seven different periods, PR in Germany has developed from the first PR departments in the political sphere (1816, 1841), which were established to influence the public opinion to the public sphere over the first 'boom phase' in the Weimar Republic (1918–1933) and the Nazi period (1933–1945), and on to professionally organized communication departments of today in big companies or political organizations. PR, which in Germany today is sometimes called the 'fifth estate', has much institutional power and can be assigned a constitutive function for Germany's democratic society.*

Keywords: German empire; Germany; Krupp; PR education and research; professionalization; (Nazi) propaganda; public relations; stratification model; Weimar Republic

Watson, Tom (ed.). *Western European Perspectives on the Development of Public Relations: Other Voices*. Basingstoke: Palgrave Macmillan, 2015. DOI: 10.1057/9781137427519.0008.

DOI: 10.1057/9781137427519.0008

Introductory and PR-historiographic remarks

The decision about when the beginning of public relations (PR) is set and how the development of PR in a country is reconstructed fundamentally depends on how 'public relations' is defined. It seems to be clear that, for example, the Roman *acta populi romani diurna* under Caesar, a newspaper-like device, was a Roman 'State Gazette', a public information device which has some similarities to today's public information newsletters (Bücher, 1922, p. 234). But there are also significant differences in the forms of government, social structures, structures of the public sphere, types of organizations between Roman society and the media systems of modern societies, particularly parliamentary democracies. To solve such problems, not flatten all differences and be able to argue a differentiated beginning of PR, the author of this chapter has developed a 'dynamic and integrated stratification model' (Bentele, 1997, 2013a,b), which proposes five coherent strata, that build upon each other. Some elements of the earlier strata remain in the later ones. PR's evolution is viewed in this model as integrative co-evolution; that is, it is seen as an integral part of the history of human communication as well as of the history of 'the public sphere'. The stratification model has an important evolutionary basis, one which until now has not been thought about or used in the history of communication. This approach is development based, since we are dealing with historical reconstructions. Differentiation and hierarchization are fundamental principles of it.

The development of PR in Germany has always been shaped and influenced by political, economic, social and technical conditions. In this context, the changing types of state had a decisive impact on German PR history: the German Alliance (1815–1866), an alliance of states of German princes and free cities, was succeeded by the German Reich (1871–1918) and the Weimar Republic (1918–1933), followed by the national–socialist dictatorship of the Third Reich, and eventually the establishment of two German states after World War II (1948), which reunited in 1990. These turning points in national history are reflected in the attempts to structure the history of German PR into periods.

A scientific German PR historiography has been emerging. However, there have already been models of distinguishing history in different periods (Bentele, 1997, 2013a, b; Avenarius, 2000; Szyszka, 2011b), many case studies (notably Binder, 1983; Döring, 1998; Zipfel 1997; Wolbring, 2000), an overview of German PR history up to 1933 (Kunczik, 1997), a

DOI: 10.1057/9781137427519.0008

volume and some articles reflecting on PR historiography (Szyszka, 1997; Liebert, 2003; Hoy, Wehmeier and Raaz, 2007; Raaz and Wehmeier, 2011a,b; Bentele, 2013a).

Bentele (1997) identified six periods of German PR history, but his recently developed model (Bentele 2013a) is a seven-period model.

Seven periods of German PR history

Periodization is the attempt to understand historical development as a sequence of phases or periods. The beginning of 'modern' PR in Germany is set at the start of the 19th century, because all criteria for 'modern public relations' are fulfilled: PR is defined by organized and full-time PR activities of an organization (e.g. a department), managing the information and communication processes between the organization and for the (internal and external) publics or stakeholders, existence of a developed media system, a public sphere (Habermas, 1990) and an occupational PR field in the strict sense. According to these criteria, modern PR can be identified in the beginning of the 19th century and, in Germany, is now over 200 years old.

The different historical periods are categorized according to criteria, such as structural changes of the political system and economic or technical criteria in later periods. Periodization in Germany leans, much more heavily than the US, on political development periods, for the reason that the development of the public sphere has also been closely tied to the development of political systems. The periodization is shown in Table 1.

TABLE 1   *Periods of German PR*

Prehistory of public relations: State press policy, 'functional' PR of emperors, kings, princes and popes; development of a set of communication instruments, procedures (campaigns) and communication strategies	
1. Period: Emergence of the an occupational/professional field (early 19th century–1918)	Activities of press relations as full-time job; development of the first press departments in politics (1816, 1841) and the economic sphere (1870); censorship; war press relations during World War I
2. Period: Consolidation and growth (1918–1933)	Rapid spread of press departments in various areas of society, the economy, politics, communal administration; first 'boom' of PR in Germany

Continued

DOI: 10.1057/9781137427519.0008

TABLE 1   *Continued*

3. Period: NS–Press Relations and political propaganda (1933–1945)	Party-ideologically dominated press relations within the framework of political propaganda; state and party control of journalism and press relations; censorship
4. Period: New beginning and upswing (1945–1958)	Post-war upswing and orientation towards American models in the early 1950s; emergence of a new professional identity in the context of democratic structures of the public sphere (PR defined as distinct from propaganda and advertising); rapid development of the professional field, particularly in the economic sphere
5. Period: Consolidation of the occupational field (1958–1985)	Federal Republic of Germany (Bundesrepublik Deutschland, BRD): Development of professional identity in the field; establishment of the professional association Deutsche Public Relations Gesellschaft (DPRG); start of non-academic, vocational training and continuing education. German Democratic Republic (GDR): Parallel to this development in the western part of Germany, beginning in the mid-1960s, the development of a party-dominated 'socialist public relations' in the GDR, with about 4000 practitioners
6. Period: Boom of the professional field, professionalization; development of academic PR research (1985–1995)	Strong development of the PR agency sector, academization and professionalization of the professional field; improvement of training, 'scientification' and professionalization of the PR toolbox, academic PR education; development of scientific research at universities
7. Period: Globalization of communication; research and education (1995– until now)	Growth of PR research and PR science, Internet: changes of the professional field through online communication and social media; professionalization (communication management; strategic communication); internationalization of the field. Further trends: quantitative increase of the field, feminization; specialization in and differentiation of the professional field.

The pre-historical period (from ancient times until the end of 18th century)

In the pre-historical period of PR, which Watson (2013, p. 3) refers to as 'proto-PR', basic organizational communication functions, such as surveillance, information, communication and persuasion (Bentele,

DOI: 10.1057/9781137427519.0008

1997), were already present, and individual communication tools that were found later as PR tools were still emerging. Craftsmen, guilds, medieval rulers, churches, political associations and their representatives engaged in communication with the aid of tools which structurally have the same or at least a similar function as the set of tools later employed by PR. Nonetheless, there is no unified phenomenon of PR as a main occupation, PR organizations (departments) or a professional field.

In this pre-historical period, many communication activities of medieval princes and emperors, kings and popes, as well as poets and writers could be located. For example, Walther von der Vogelweide (1170–1230), the most important German-language poet of the Middle Ages, worked as a political poet in the service of Philip of Swabia, Otto IV and Frederick II. He earned his living through political poetry in which he praised his masters or criticized the Pope. Michael Kunczik (1997, p. 30) classified him as the 'first full-time propagandist'.

The communicative self-presentation of the (German) Hanseatic League, the association of Low German merchants of the mid-12th century to the 17th century, was based on the systematic use of communication tools, such as representative buildings and customs. The communication instruments of the very wealthy Fugger trading and banking family, that is their 'Fuggerzeitungen' (Fugger newspapers), are an early example of a correspondent network during the 16th century. The Fugger family received not only business news from their correspondents, but also sensationalist and gossip news (Kleinpaul, 1922).

The first period (beginning of the 19th century until 1918)

The first period, which can be called 'development of the profession', starts in the early 19th century and ends at the close of World War I in 1918. The earliest organized activities can be observed in the sphere of politics (governments, ministries), the economic sphere (companies) and the sphere of associations (trade associations, labour unions etc.) followed later. The cradle of modern German PR can be located in the time of the Prussian reforms after 1807. Writers such as William Wekhrlin and Julius Lange were already active as publicists and as state employees in the 1790s, Karl August Varnhagen von Ense was working as a full-time 'press officer', hired by the Prussian Chancellor von Hardenberg during

DOI: 10.1057/9781137427519.0008

the Vienna Congress (1813–1814). Varnhagen von Ense briefly had the duty to influence public opinion (Hofmeister-Hunger, 1994, p. 284). In 1816, the first 'Literary Bureau' was established and led by Friedrich von Cölln (ibid., p. 372). The institutionalization of PR and a professional field had begun. The duties of the office were similar to today's press department: systematic surveillance of the press, writing of articles and communication with journalists in order to influence public opinion on behalf of, and for, the benefit of the Prussian government. But there was also another duty: censorship, which was not completely abolished until the end of World War I in 1918. Another important instrument of the 'press politics' (equivalent to 'public relations') of the Prussian government to influence the public opinion was the establishment of 'official' newspapers, such as the *Allgemeine Preußische Staatszeitung* (General Prussian state newspaper). It was founded, at the same time as two other private newspapers in Berlin in 1819, with the task of influencing public opinion.

In 1841, the Ministerial-Zeitungsbüro (governmental bureau of newspapers) was established in Prussia, as a political institution to 'correct' wrong press reports – the impression of censorship was overtly avoided (Nöth-Greis, 1997). After the official abolition of censorship in 1848, the functions of the succeeding institutions, such as Literarisches Cabinet (Literary Cabinet) (1848–1859), Centralstelle für Presseangelegenheiten (Central office of Press Affairs) (1850–1860) and Literarisches Büro (Literary Bureau) (1860–1920), shifted to observation of the press, internal information within the Prussian government and international press relations. Particularly under Reichschancellor Bismarck this shift included more subtle influence and control of the press. For example, 'official' (government-friendly) newspapers were financially supported (Nöth-Greis, 1997; Koszyk, 1966). This practice of government 'holding the reins' of the press continued after the founding of the German Reich and after the liberalization of the press through the Reich press law.

One of the most important public campaigns in the German Reich was Admiral Alfred von Tirpitz's 'fleet campaign' (Deist, 1976; Bollenbach, 2009). The politically motivated extension of the fleet was disguised with economic explanations and propagated through posters, lectures and press reports (Kunczik, 1997). However, PR activities at the local and municipal level were less manipulative. They mostly focused on developing and maintaining relationships with local publics and carrying on the tasks of the cities, thereby performing community relations (Liebert, 1995).

DOI: 10.1057/9781137427519.0008

Besides the political changes of the 19th century, economic and technical progress also shaped PR's development. Coal mining and the steel industry were pivotal foundations of heavy industry, while electronics and chemistry became innovative growth industries. Alfred Krupp, Emil Rathenau and Werner von Siemens simultaneously became leading businessmen as well as architects of PR in the 19th century (Zipfel, 1997; Wolbring, 2000). A prime example was the Krupp steel factory founded in 1821. Alfred Krupp, the son of the founder, took over management after his father's death in 1826. The corporate communication of the company began with personal letters and visits to customers. However, from as early as the 1820s, the company participated in trade exhibitions. In 1851, Alfred Krupp managed a coup that secured worldwide awareness, recognition and an excellent reputation as a producer of quality steel: the exhibition of a 2.5-ton steel block, the largest block of cast steel of the time. It was followed by the early use of communication tools, such as printed business cards, photography and other means. In 1870, a first full-time 'Literat' (man of letters) was employed, who was responsible for Krupp's corporate communications.

In the course of industrialization, friction developed between powerful organizations, including wealthy business families, and the evolving working class. Along with industrialization and urbanization, social hardship appeared that demanded response from politicians and businesses. Consequently, the late 19th century witnessed the first steps towards social legislation and the first efforts at human relations, such as employee magazines, pensions, sports and singing clubs, and recreation homes for children. The motivation for these moves originated from the ethical pretence of numerous businessmen viewing themselves as 'fathers of a family of workers' on the one hand, while fearing strikes and rebellions on the other (Gall, 2000; Wehler, 1995).

In addition to these internal communication practices, there were early accounts of external communication instruments in companies, such as AEG, Siemens, Krupp. The so-called *Literaten* were employed to observe and influence the press. AEG had already begun to systematically analyze the press clippings (Zipfel, 1997).

The second period (1918–1933)

The second period was a time of consolidation and growth that covers the Weimar Republic (1918–1933). It testified to new social conditions: a

DOI: 10.1057/9781137427519.0008

parliamentary–democratic form of government and an economically independent and active press that was no longer controlled by the state. The press departments of companies and associations developed rapidly. Communal press relations, which began with the establishment of the first municipal press office in Magdeburg in 1906, had taken on an organizational form. It had become, just as with the press relations of state institutions, more important in the new democratic forms and was significantly expanded: the first 'boom-period' of German PR. Because of the economic boom of the 'Golden Twenties', not only the state but more and more companies and associations recognized the necessity and use of PR (Kunczik, 1997).

Evidence is provided in an article by Kurt Tucholsky from 1920, who critically and ironically commented on this boom in press offices:

> These press offices spread like rabbits after the war as an army of writers, unfit for war and life, of spectacle men, of recorders, of hack writers and office clerks flowed, jobless, over Germany, were out of work ... Every theatre, every government office and every battalion of uniformed idlers has its own public relations office. The public relations office is commanded either by a journalist or by an otherwise unemployed officer. It consists of two typewriters each, eight female typists, two journalists, a recorder – and is founded on fear of the press. (Tucholsky, 1920/1990, p. 211)

PR's expansion in the Weimar Republic was an important period in German PR history in that, for the first time, the practice became possible under the conditions of a democratic public sphere. These conditions changed suddenly with the takeover of political power by the Nazis.

The third period: National Socialism propaganda and press relations

The time of National Socialism (1933–1945), which was co-terminous with the third period of German PR history (1933–1945), represented a step backwards for public communication. Under the Nazi dictatorship, the media were brought in line and exploited to advance the Nazi doctrine. The national–socialist state made great propagandistic efforts and the oppressed media (press, broadcasting and film) served as 'loudspeakers' of political and ideological content. While there had existed a relatively diverse and independent media system in the Weimar Republic, public information activities under the Nazis were centralized under the 'Reichsministerium für Voksaufklärung und Propaganda' (Reich Ministry of Public Information

DOI: 10.1057/9781137427519.0008

and Propaganda) with Propaganda Minister Josef Goebbels on top (Sösemann, 2011). The media were cleared of Jewish journalists and strict penalties were introduced to punish people who did not write stories that pleased the Nazis. Needless to say, the entire system of public communication gained a propagandistic character. Although external media relations and internal information of governmental organizations, associations, communities, cultural institutions and companies still existed during the Nazi dictatorship, these activities often employed a propagandistic communication style. During this period, German pioneers Carl Hundhausen (Lehming, 1997) and Albert Oeckl (Bentele, 2005; Mattke, 2006) got their first experience in PR (called Öffentlichkeitsarbeit) and advertising.

The fourth period (1945–1958): new beginning and upswing

After 1945, in the early phase of economic and political reconstruction, there were several years during which press relations of some organizations may have been carried on here and there, but the wider development of PR began only in the early 1950s. The first publications on PR appeared in 1951 (Gross, 1951; Hundhausen, 1951). In the following years, there was reorientation and an altered democratic self-image of PR, and also indications of its quantitative expansion. PR, in the context of a parliamentary democracy, not only had to redefine itself but it also had to distance its practices clearly from (Nazi) propaganda. Separation from advertising was also important in defining PR's role and purpose. During this fourth period, the orientation towards the American model was important because of the Allied occupation and its link with democratic principles. From today's perspective, it is notable that during the 12 years of National Socialism the ties to the press relations experiences of the Weimar Republic had broken off completely. This could be observed in terms of personnel as well as at the level of the PR literature of the time.

The fifth period (1958–1985): consolidation of the field and the 'Socialist Öffentlichkeitsarbeit' in the GDR

The year 1958, when the Deutsche Public Relations Gesellschaft [German Public Relations Association] (DPRG) was established (on 8 December

DOI: 10.1057/9781137427519.0008

in Bonn), marked the beginning of the fifth period and can be described as 'consolidation of the field'. During this period the professional field started to form nationally; regional discussion circles (e.g. in the Hamburg region), which existed before DPRG's founding, were carried on nationally concerning the profession's self-image, for example, through annual conferences. The reflection of the professional field by practitioners had begun. The existence of the DPRG enabled systematic professional exchanges, nationwide discussions and activities concerning PR training and other issues of importance to the professional field as a whole. This was a phase of continual expansion of professionally run PR activities, quantitative growth and stabilization of self-image. Non-academic training institutions, initiated by the professional association and private individuals, were set up and helped in the recruiting and continuing education of the new generation of PR professionals. The first PR agency was established in 1952, other agencies followed in the 1950s before this field became much stronger from the 1960s onwards (Nöthe, 1994).

In the Soviet-controlled German Democratic Republic (GDR), a type of 'sozialistische Öffentlichkeitsarbeit' (socialist PR) developed from the mid-1960s, which was ideologically distinct from the West. As was the case during the Nazi period, it would be too simplistic and inconsistent to assume that only political propaganda existed in the GDR. Not only did the professional field of 'public relations' really exist, which, according to information provided by practitioners, made up some 3000–4000 individuals, but there were several normative regulations on the shaping of socialist PR, a discussion in the context of scholarship, and scholarly inspired descriptions of the practical activity at the time. 'Socialist public relations' in the GDR in the cultural sphere, at the Leipzig trade fair, in mass organizations and also in the area of production was carried on as a practical activity; operating under the rules of the political-propaganda system and conditions of socialism. Nevertheless, it was a professional activity that was clearly distinguishable from journalism, advertising and state-driven political propaganda (Bentele, 2008).

The sixth period (1985–1995): boom of the professional field, beginning of university education and research

In the mid-1980s, the professional field of PR in the Federal Republic started to boom. The sixth period of German PR development is presented

DOI: 10.1057/9781137427519.0008

in this section. PR agencies developed rapidly; the German association of public relations agencies (German acronym: GPRA), established in 1972, took a leadership and management role in the PR agency sector. With several activities that extended well beyond the more narrowly defined professional field of PR (e.g. the AIDS campaign commissioned by the German Federal Centre for Health Education), broader initiatives were undertaken that drew attention to the PR sector as a whole. Membership of the professional association rose strongly from the mid-1980s and the percentage of DPRG members who had an academic diploma rose from some 30 per cent in the mid-1980s to over 60 per cent in the early 1990s. Training activities became more intensive and, from early in the 1990s, in the field of communication science, PR became a topic in university education and research. A new organization was established in 1987: the Deutsche Rat für Public Relations (German council of public relations), an ethical organization of self-control for the field, which looks continuously at practitioner behaviour and can issue public reprimands (Avenarius and Bentele, 2009). Academic PR education began to develop contours and the continually practiced science of PR emerged. In 1994, the first chair for PR in the German-speaking countries was established at the University of Leipzig and the first university PR programmes were developed in Leipzig, Berlin, Hannover and many other universities. All this contributed to a professionalization of the field, a process which, however, cannot yet be considered complete.

The seventh period (1995–until now): Internet, social media, further professionalization

The seventh period of the German PR history (1995–until now) is characterized by the global development of the Internet and thus of online PR, as well as by changes that have occurred through the social media. For communication departments of international companies, 24-hours-a-day, seven-days-a-week operation is normal. An increasing acceleration of the external and internal communication can be observed. A new professional association, the Deutsche Pressesprecherverband (German association for spokespeople), founded in 2003 developed rapidly and is now (2014) the biggest PR association in Germany with 4300 members. In general, it is estimated, that at least 50,000 full-time practitioners are working in the field. The development of communication departments,

DOI: 10.1057/9781137427519.0008

particularly in large international companies, into highly professional, strategically operating departments can be observed. The professionalization of crisis communication, issues management, PR evaluation and communication controlling as well as the communication of corporate social responsibility policies and actions are further characteristics. Communication by organizations has become more regulated with companies introducing written rules, even where there are few legal provisions, such as in the financial sector. An example is press relations where, coordinated with the compliance departments, procedures have been introduced because of public criticism of the communication behaviour of those companies. PR researchers in Germany cooperate with the communication managers of big companies. Research at universities is not only oriented at basic research, but also in application-oriented research, which for both sides (science and industry) is a positive relationship. Feminization of the profession is, in addition to professionalization and 'scientization', an important characteristic.

Final remarks

The history of PR in Germany in the previous 210 years points to the institutionalization of a profession and formation of a professional field, which today not only has great appeal for young people, but also has clear contours with its professional organizations, higher education paths and an ethical dimension of reflection. PR also has important social functions: without the continuous PR activities of organizations, journalism and the media systems could not exist. PR informs the society about a wide range of topics, bringing diverse opinions into the public discourse. PR thus can be assigned a constitutive function for Germany's democratic society.

References

Avenarius, H. (2000) *Public Relations. Die Grundform der gesellschaftlichen Kommunikation* [Public Relations. The Basic Form of Societal Communication], 2nd edition (Darmstadt: Wiss. Buchgesellschaft).
Avenarius, H. and Bentele, G. (eds) (2009) *Selbstkontrolle im Berufsfeld Public Relations. Reflexionen und Dokumentation* [Self-Control

DOI: 10.1057/9781137427519.0008

in the Professional Field of Public Relations. Reflections and Documentation] (Wiesbaden: VS Verlag für Sozialwissenschaften).

Bentele, G. (1997) 'PR-Historiographie und funktional-integrative Schichtung. Ein neuer Ansatz zur PR-Geschichtsschreibung' [PR-Historiography and a Functional-Integrative Stratification], in P. Szyszka (ed.) *Auf der Suche nach einer Identität. PR-Geschichte als Theoriebaustein* [In Search of an Identity. PR History as Theory Building Block] (Berlin: Vistas).

Bentele, G. (2005) 'Oeckl, Albert', in R. L. Heath (ed.) *Encyclopedia of Public Relations* (Thousand Oaks, CA: Sage).

Bentele, G. (2008) 'Sozialistische Öffentlichkeitsarbeit in der DDR' [Socialist Public Relations in the GDR], in G. Bentele, R. Fröhlich and P. Szyszka (eds) *Handbuch Public Relations. Wissenschaftliche Grundlagen und berufliches Handeln. Mit Lexikon* [Handbook of Public Relations. Scientific Principles and Professional Actions, with Encyclopedia] (Wiesbaden: VS Verlag für Sozialwissenschaften).

Bentele, G. (2013a) 'Der Diskurs über PR-Geschichte und PR-Historiographie in Deutschland und international' [The Discourse about PR History and PR Historiography in Germany and International], in O. Hoffjann and S. Huck-Sandhu (eds) *UnVergessene Diskurse. 20 Jahre PR- und Organisationskommunikationsforschung* [Unforgotten Discourses. 20 Years Research about Public Relations and Organizational Communication] (Wiesbaden: Springer VS).

Bentele, G. (2013b) 'Public Relations Historiography: Perspectives of a Functional-Integrative Stratification Model', in K. Sriramesh, A. Zerfass and J-N Kim (eds) *Current Trends and Emerging Topics in Public Relations and Communication Management* (New York: Routledge).

Bentele, G. and Wehmeier, S. (2009) 'From Literary Bureaus to a Modern Profession: The Development and Current Structure of Public Relations in Germany', in K. Sriramesh and D. Verčič (eds) *The Global Public Relations Handbook. Theory, Research and Practice.* Expanded and Revised edition (New York: Routledge).

Binder, E. (1983) *Die Entstehung unternehmerischer Public Relations in der Bundesrepublik Deutschland* [The Development of Corporate Public Relations in the Federal Republic of Germany] (Münster: Lit Verlag).

Bollenbach, A. (2009) 'Erzwungene Professionalisierung? Eine Analyse staatlicher Öffentlichkeitsarbeit im deutschen Kaiserreich 1890–1914 am Beispiel der „Flottenpropaganda" [Forced Professionalization?

DOI: 10.1057/9781137427519.0008

An Analysis of State Public Relations during the German Empire
1890–1914. The Example of the 'Fleet Propaganda'], unpublished
Master's thesis (Universität Leipzig, Germany).

Bücher, K. (1922) *Die Entstehung der Volkswirtschaft, Vorträge undAufsätze*
[The Development of the National Economy. Lectures and Essays]
(Tübingen: Verlag der H. Lauppschen Buchhandlung).

Deist, W. (1976) *Flottenpolitik und Flottenpropaganda. Das
Nachrichtenbureau des Reichs-marineamtes 1897–1914* [Fleet Policy and
Fleet Propaganda. The News Bureau of the German Imperial Naval
Office] (Stuttgart: Deutsche Verlags-Anstalt).

Döring, U. (1998) *Die Öffentlichkeitsarbeit der Evangelischen Kirche in
Deutschland. Eine Bestandsaufnahme* [The Public Relations of the
Protestant Church in Germany. An Inventory], unpublished doctoral
thesis (Universität Leipzig, Germany).

Gall, L. (2000) *Krupp. Der Aufstieg eines Industrieimperiums* [Krupp. The
Rise of an Industrial Empire] (Berlin: Siedler).

Gross, H. (1951) *Moderne Meinugspflege* [Modern Maintenance/
Cultivation of Public Opinion] (Düsseldorf: Droste).

Habermas, J. (1990) *The Structural Transformation of the Public Sphere.
an Inquiry into a Category of Bourgeois Society* (Cambridge, Mass:
MIT Press) [originally published in 1962 as *Strukturwandel der
Öffentlichkeit. Untersuchungen zu einer Kategorie der bürgerlichen
Gesellschaft* (Darmstadt and Neuwied: Luchterhand Verlag)].

Hofmeister-Hunger, A. (1994) *Pressepolitik und Staatsreform. Die
Institutionalisierung staatlicher Öffentlichkeitsarbeit bei August
von Hardenberg (1792–1822)* [Press Policy and State Reform. The
Institutionalization of State Public Relations of August von
Hardemberg (1792–1822] (Göttingen: Vandenhoek & Ruprecht).

Hoy, P., Wehmeier, S. and Raaz, O. (2007) 'From Facts to Stories or
from Stories to Facts? Analysing Public Relations History in Public
Relations Textbooks', *Public Relations Review*, 33, 191–200.

Hundhausen, C. (1951) *Werbung um öffentliches Vertrauen. Public Relations*
[Advertising for Public Trust. Public Relations] (Essen: Girardet).

Kleinpaul, J. (1922) *Die Fuggerzeitungen 1568–1605* [The Fugger Papers
1568–1605] (Leipzig: Reinicke) (Reprinted 1972 by Martin Sändig,
Wiesbaden).

Koszyk, K. (1966) *Deutsche Presse im 19. Jahrhundert. Geschichte der
deutschen Presse* [German Press in 19th Century. History of the
German Press] (Berlin: Colloquium Verlag).

DOI: 10.1057/9781137427519.0008

Kunczik, M. (1997) *Geschichte der Öffentlichkeitsarbeit in Deutschland* [The History of Public Relations in Germany] (Köln, Weimar, Wien: Böhlau).

Lehming, E-M. (1997) *Carl Hundhausen: sein Leben, sein Werk, sein Lebenswerk. Public Relations in Deutschland* [Carl Hundhausen: His Life, His Work, His Lifework. Public Relations in Germany] (Wiesbaden: DUV).

Liebert, T. (1995) 'History of Municipal Public Relations in Germany (from Its Roots Up to the Weimar Republic)', Paper presented at the International Public Relations Research Symposium, Lake Bled, Slovenia, 6–9 July 1995.

Liebert, T. (2003) *Der Take-off von Öffentlichkeitsarbeit* [The Take-Off of Public Relations] (Leipzig: University of Leipzig).

Mattke, C. (2006) *Albert Oeckl. Sein Leben und Wirken für die deutsche Öffentlichkeitsarbeit* [Albert Oeckl. His Life and His Work for German Public Relations] (Wiesbaden: VS Verlag für Sozialwissenschaften).

Nöthe, B. (1994) *PR-Agenturen in der Bundesrepublik Deutschland* [PR Agencies in Germany] (Münster: Agenda).

Nöth-Greis, G. (1997) 'Das Literarische Büro als Instrument der Pressepolitik' [The Literary Bureau as Instrument of Press Policy], in J. Wilke (ed.) *Pressepolitik und Propaganda. Historische Studien vom Vormärz bis zum Kalten Krieg* [Press Policy and Propaganda. Historical Studies from Vormärz [The Time before the 1848 March Revolution] Until Cold War] (Köln: Böhlau).

Raaz, O., and Wehmeier, S. (2011a) 'Histories of Public Relations. Comparing the Historiography of British, German and US Public Relations', *Journal of Communication Management*, 15(3), 256–275.

Raaz, O. and Wehmeier, S. (2011b) 'Unsichere PR-Geschichte: PR-Historiographien im systematischen Vergleich' [Unsecure PR history: PR Historiographies in a Systematic Comparison], *medien & zeit*, 26(1), 6–15.

Sösemann, B. (2011) *Propaganda. Medien und Öffentlichkeit in der NS-Diktatur. In Zusammenarbeit mit Marius Lange*, 2 Bde [Propaganda. Media and the Public Sphere in NS Dictatorship. In cooperation with Marius Lange] (Stuttgart: Franz Steiner Verlag).

Sriramesh, K. and Verčič, D. (eds) (2009) *The Global Public Relations Handbook. Theory, Research and Practice.* Expanded and Revised edition (New York: Routledge).

DOI: 10.1057/9781137427519.0008

Szyszka, P. (2011a) 'Deutsche PR-Nachkriegsgeschichte als Berufsfeldgeschichte. Ein revidiertes Phasenmodell' [German PR-History after World War II. a Revised Phase Model]. *medien & zeit*, 26(1), 39–53.

Szyszka, P. (2011b) 'Vom Wiener Kongress bis zur Weimarer Republik. Die Frühgeschichte deutscher PR-Arbeit aus theoriegestützter Perspektive' [From the Congress of Vienna to Weimar Republic. Early History of German PR from a Theoretically Supported Perspective], *medien & zeit*, 26(1), 16–29.

Szyszka, P. (ed.) (1997) *Auf der Suche nach einer Identität. PR-Geschichte als Theoriebaustein* [In Search of Identity. PR History as Building Stone for PR-Theory] (Berlin: Vistas).

Tucholsky, K. (1920) 'Pressestellen' [Press Departments], *Freiheit* 8 August 1920. Reprinted in Tucholsky, K. (1990) *Deutsches Tempo. Texte 1911 bis 1932*. [German Tempo. Texts 1911 until 1932], edited by M. Gerold-Tucholsky and F. J. Raddatz (Reinbek: Rowohlt).

Watson, T. (2013) 'Keynote Paper', presented at the International History of Public Relations Conference, Bournemouth, UK, 24 June 2013.

Wehler, H.-U. (1995) *Deutsche Gesellschaftsgeschichte 1849–1914*. [German Social History 1849–1914] (München: C. H. Beck).

Wehmeier, S., Raaz, O. and Hoy, P. (2009) 'PR-Geschichten. Ein systematischer Vergleich der PR-Historiographie in Deutschland und den USA' [PR Histories. A Systematic Comparison of PR Historiographies in Germany and USA], in A. Averbeck-Lietz, P. Klein and M. Meyen (eds) *Historische und Systematische Kommunikationswissenschaft. Festschrift für Arnulf Kutsch* [Historical and Systematic Communication Science. Festschrift for Arnulf Kutsch] (Bremen: edition lumiére).

Wolbring, B. (2000) *Krupp und die Öffentlichkeit im 19. Jahrhundert: Selbstdarstellung, öffentliche Wahrnehmung und gesellschaftliche Kommunikation* [Krupp and the Public Sphere. Self-Presentation, Public Perception and Societal Communication] (München: C. H. Beck).

Zipfel, A. (1997) *Public Relations in der Elektroindustrie. Die Firma Siemens und AEG 1847 bis 1939* [Public Relations in the Electricity Industry. Siemens and AEG from 1847 until 1939] (Köln: Böhlau).

DOI: 10.1057/9781137427519.0008

5

Greece

Anastasios Theofilou

Abstract: *This chapter aims to present the evolution of PR in Greece from the early 1950s until today by outlining historic developments, main actors, international influences, professional bodies and obstacles that Greek PR has faced over the years.*

Keywords: Greece; history of public relations; IPRA; public relations

Watson, Tom (ed.). *Western European Perspectives on the Development of Public Relations: Other Voices*. Basingstoke: Palgrave Macmillan, 2015. DOI: 10.1057/9781137427519.0009.

DOI: 10.1057/9781137427519.0009

The geopolitical situation of Greece has had a major influence on the country's historic evolution and economic development. Greece (or to be more precise Hellas) is a country of 11 million people located at the crossroads between Europe and Asia, at the 'powder keg of Europe' (i.e. Balkan peninsula) and, according to the Yalta conference in 1945, 'belongs to the West'. Focusing only on conflicts since the beginning of the 20th century, Greece was involved in the 'Macedonian Struggle' (1904–1908), both Balkan Wars (1912–1913), World War I (1914–1918), World War II (1939–1945), while the Civil War (1946–1949) and the military junta (1967–1974) should also be acknowledged. Without attempting to evaluate the psychological effects on its population, these conflicts drained the country's resources and led to an infrastructural and economical gap compared with other Western European counties. The major attempt to cover this gap started after World War II when Greece received financial support and was offered 'know-how' by former war allies (mainly the United States). Being on the victor's side in all war conflicts Greece has had a series of diplomatic achievements, such as becoming member of numerous institutions, among which are the North Atlantic Treaty Organization (NATO) in 1952 and the European Economic Community (EEC, predecessor of the European Union) in 1981.

Birth and major historic developments from 1951 until today

In an attempt to promote Greece as a tourist destination to the developed countries, such as France, Germany, UK and US, the Greek National Tourism Organization (EOT) appointed the US-owned advertising agency Foote, Cone and Belding on a six-month contract in 1951 (IoC, 2003; Magkliveras, 1970). This was to be the first time that the term 'public relations' (PR) was officially used (Magkliveras, 1970; Zobanakis, 1974; Coutoupis, 1992; IoC, 2003, 2004; Theofilou and Watson, 2014). The manager of this campaign was a British PR adviser Eric Williams who worked with Manos Pavlidis, who was to become the 'father' of Greek PR (Coutoupis, 1992; IoC, 2003). The collaboration was initiated between Williams and ADEL, the most reputed Greek advertising agency of the time. ADEL was co-founded by Pavlidis and leading advertising personality Chrysostomos Papadopoulos (ibid.). According to Andrew Rizopoulos (a leading Greek PR personality who practiced

DOI: 10.1057/9781137427519.0009

until the early 1980s), 'Pavlidis is the father of PR, while ADEL is the mother' (A. Rizopoulos, personal communication, 13 June 2013).

The term 'public relations' is found in organizational documents for the first time in the mid-1950s at the Public Power Corporation SA (DEH) (IoC, 2003). Back then it was Embasco consultancy advising on the formation of the role/department; however, the term was translated inaccurately at the time to 'Dimosies Sxeseis' (which is a literal translation for 'Public Relations'), causing a confusion about the true meaning and value of the concept (Papamichalakis, 1961; Magkliveras, 1970; Tsiligiannis, 1973; IoC, 2003; Rizopoulos, personal communication) The specific translation does not capture the humanitarian and relationship value of the concept (Theofilou and Watson, 2014).

As there were no PR experts at that time and only a couple of PR agencies, the translation of the term was not challenged rigorously (Rizopoulos, personal communication). The limited number of PR agencies had another consequence for the development of PR in Greece. As international companies started to seek collaboration in the country, the turn to advertising agencies as the first point of contact was inevitable (R. Malikouti, personal communication, 10 June 2013). Hence, as the new profession was just forming, PR was unavoidably linked to advertising agencies causing further confusion to Greek clients who couldn't understand the difference between advertising and PR and kept requesting that PR practitioners implement advertising tactics for them (IoC, 2004). As a result, the PR market was strongly linked with advertising agencies. This was not unnoticed by the PR pioneers who sustained their relationships with advertising agencies. Pavlidis founded his PR agency 'Desmos' in 1957/1958 and kept working closely with ADEL, while another pioneer Marcel Yoel went as far as to establish a subsidiary advertising agency to complement his PR business (ibid.).

The need to learn, educate, create awareness and establish the new profession led to the foundation of the Hellenic Public Relations Association (HPRA) in 1960 (Zobanakis, 1974; Rizopoulos, personal communication) and the foundation of the Hellenic Public Relations Association of North Greece shortly after (Bokouvou, 1974). According to Watson (2011), HPRA gained recognition by the International Public Relations Association (IPRA) in the same year (Hague Council Minutes, 1960, p. 9) thus becoming the first point of reference for foreign companies/clients who wanted to operate in Greece and IPRA (Malikouti, personal communication). Appreciating the importance of international

DOI: 10.1057/9781137427519.0009

exposure and reputation in the period from 1960 to 1980, Pavlidis and Yoel undertook high-level responsibilities within IPRA (Watson, 2011; Theofilou and Watson, 2014). Another reason that Greek PR pioneers of the time turned to IPRA (or the UK's Institute of Public Relations in Rizopoulos's case) to expand their network internationally could have been the seven-year-long military dictatorship from 1967 to 1974. Even though a fundamental principle of practicing PR is freedom of speech, it appears that the junta did not affect the PR industry's development at the time (M. Yoel, personal communication, 12 June 2013; Rizopoulos, personal communication 2013).

The beginning of the 1980s may be considered the peak of Greek PR's active involvement with IPRA. During the European Confederation of Public Relations (CERP) annual conference in Athens in 1980, HPRA celebrated the 15 years since IPRA's Code of Athens was adopted in the Greek capital and gave an award to the 'father' of European PR, Lucien Matrat, for his authorship of the Code (Theofilou and Watson, 2014). The Greek representatives appreciated the value in Matrat's development of a Code of ethical standards and were among those who prominently supported it. HPRA and Greek PR practitioners (especially those with active IPRA involvement) saw the naming of the Code (i.e. Code of Athens) and the event organized in Athens in 1980 as a victory for Greek PR and recognition of its professional status.

Despite the promising start and the era of optimism that followed as Greece became the tenth member of the EEC, PR practitioners in the post-1980 era did not have successors of equal standing as the pioneers (Coutoupis, 1992). The rapid expansion of the profession and attempts to enlarge HPRA did not have the anticipated results and did not strengthen the substance of Greek PR. On the contrary, many major personalities of the time alienated themselves from HPRA (Malikouti, personal communication; Yoel, personal communication; Rizopoulos, personal communication; T. Coutoupis, personal communication, 9 September 2014). It could have also been that PR practitioners did not appreciate the value of actively following international developments as multinational companies (e.g. Shell, Mobil) and international PR agency groups (e.g. Burson-Marsteller, Hill & Knowlton, Ogilvy) were already operating in Greece. In the period before the 1980, the relationship with IPRA was mainly for personal benefit which gave access to a wider market. Considering the difficulties faced with local clients, the international involvement was necessary for business and professional development,

DOI: 10.1057/9781137427519.0009

which was the strategy of the two main personalities of the pre-1980s era. Pavlidis, followed by Yoel, were the first to see this necessity to expand their network internationally and so became actively involved with IPRA (Theofilou and Watson, 2014). Coutoupis and Malikouti (major personalities of the post-1980s era) followed their lead and, as the Greek IPRA representatives in the 1980s and 1990s respectively, managed to keep the membership numbers high; however, the members' participation and interest was not as active as in the past (Malikouti, personal communication). Changes in the operational structure of IPRA especially in the post-1990 era also did not help the case for Greece (ibid.).

The financial prosperity of the late 1990s led to the reorganization of the Hellenic Association of Advertising Agencies (EDEE founded in 1968) in 2000 to become the Hellenic Association of Advertising and Communication Agencies (EDEE, keeping the same acronym), which is also its current form. This historic turning point was necessary as PR did not have a professional body that was as active as HPRA had been in the 1960s. From 2000 the professional body of EDEE was divided into five sectors (namely, Advertising, PR, Media Specialists, Integrated Marketing Communications and Branding and Design) with the PR sector being for agencies operating in the fields of PR, public affairs, sponsorship and events marketing (Hellenic Association of Advertising and Communication Agencies, 2014).

Finally, in 2002, before the first signs of the economic crisis which was to follow the 2004 Olympic Games and still experiencing (with a lag) the stock exchange crisis of 1999, EDEE founded the Institute of Communication (IoC) with a clear vision to support PR education and to offer a link between academia and professional practice. In the years which followed the formation of IoC, numerous positive efforts have been made to develop a Greek PR archive and educate PR practitioners; even though the 2008 economic crisis has been limiting these efforts if not completely blocking them.

International influences

When considering the development of PR in Greece, the international influences from Britain, France and, mainly, the US are evident. When the term 'public relations' was initially introduced, it was part of a project assigned to a US advertising agency funded by the Marshall Plan, even

DOI: 10.1057/9781137427519.0009

though the funds were eventually reallocated to military purposes (Theofilou and Watson, 2014). The know-how of a new profitable discipline came from North America as did the literature, which became the main reference for those who wanted to expand their knowledge and educate themselves about PR. Pavlidis (IoC, 2003) and Rizopoulos (personal communication) have commented that the vast majority of the literature was in English (inferring the US). This was also confirmed by the author's desk research where it was observed that the reference indexes of most books written in Greek (from 1950s until today) included books mainly written in English by US authors and with acknowledgment to Ivy L. Lee and Edward L. Bernays as those who first started practicing PR. US literature and practice dominated from 1951 to 1960s. After the 1960s, there was a turn towards the European school of thought. Involvement with IPRA and the 'philosopher' of European PR, Lucien Matrat, offered a different perspective which resulted in Greek PR being a blend of US and European school of thought fused with national cultural perspectives.

According to Rizopoulos (personal communication), the US approach, more business-oriented, was adopted easily by many practitioners. Similarly multinational companies, such as Mobil and Shell operating in Greece, offered a practical learning experience to those involved with their established 'in-house' PR. Because of the lack of national PR educational programmes, the multinational organizations complemented what Greek practitioners learned through their own experiences and personal readings. Two of the most influential personalities of the post-1980s era, Thalis Coutoupis and Rita Malikouti, were deeply involved with PR programmes developed by multinational companies (Malikouti, personal communication; Coutoupis, personal communication).

The international influences were also brought into the Greek market by major PR agency networks, such as Ketchum, Hill & Knowlton, Burson-Marsteller (to name a few) which collaborated with Greek PR agencies/practitioners either to overcome legal obstacles (most commonly the issue before the 1980s) or to better understand the culture of country and unique attributes of the market.

Professional bodies

IPRA had a strong presence in Greece until the early 2000s. The relationship that leading pioneers developed before the 1980s laid the

DOI: 10.1057/9781137427519.0009

ground for their successors, such as Coutoupis and Malikouti, to sustain the link. However, as it was personal interest and ambition that made IPRA have such a strong impact on Greek PR life in the pre-1980s era, this interest weakened in the 1980s and 1990s era (Malikouti, personal communication; Rizopoulos, personal communication; Yoel, personal communication). Alongside IPRA's reorganization and the change of the Greek market after entering EEC, the relationship between Greek PR and IPRA faded (Malikouti, personal communication).

HPRA remains the professional body of PR in Greece even though in 2000 PR became officially a division of EDEE. According to Coutoupis (personal communication), HPRA carried on operating until its 2007 assembly after which it became apparent to him that HPRA could not carry on. Despite indications that HPRA is still officially active, it is EDEE which has become the first point of reference when researching PR. EDEE has been a full member of the International Communications Consultancy Organization (ICCO) since 2001.

Field of practice

PR has been practiced widely and differently in various fields, which can be expected given the different backgrounds of the practitioners. Rizopoulos identifies four main PR functions until the early 1990s (Rizopoulos, personal communication):

▶ The first function was to offer consultancy by reporting directly to an organization's CEO, in the same manner as other functions. Rizopoulos identified the international influences of US literature, including later Excellence approaches (Grunig et al., 1992). As most Greek companies did not have internal PR departments, or knew little about PR, the norm was to outsource to a consultant or an agency. The PR agency or consultant thus reported directly to the CEO (or owner) of the company as in the examples of companies such as IZOLA, Minion and Peiraiki-Patraiki.
▶ The second function, propaganda, was related to the communication and relationship outcome that ministries and state organizations sought. Given the country's profile, political propaganda was an activity that must be explored separately.
▶ The third function was to develop and sustain relationships with the press. Rizopoulos identified two patterns of professional

DOI: 10.1057/9781137427519.0009

practice when cultivating press relations: In the first case practitioners would make the press release part of a wider advertising plan acting in a sense as advertisers, while the second was former journalists making their way into PR mainly because of their media practice background (i.e. knowledge, writing skills and existing network).

▸ The fourth function, marketing PR, came later when compared with the other three and was widely used especially after the 1980s. In the case of 'Marketing PR' it becomes apparent that PR was perceived as an element of marketing.

Following Rizopoulos's categorization, the developments of the field of practice can be identified in locally published literature. Greek literature before the 1980s focused mainly on understanding the new discipline by adopting (if not translating) literature written in English, and occasionally French, and attempting to express it in the Greek context. This approach demonstrated that Greeks were not just copying US practices. Indicatively: Papamichalakis (1961) places human relations in the heart of PR while discussing cases of the banking industry; Bokovou (1974) links PR to the modern economy; Magkliveras (1970) following Papamichalakis attempts to identify PR elements in the campaign organized by the Greek Church for the celebration of the Apostle Paul; Zobanakis (1965) and Magkliveras (1965) put PR in a more political context discussing the value of democracy and freedom of speech; while Pavlidis was thanked and referenced nearly by everyone for his contribution to the field. Pavlidis wrote about PR in magazines and newspapers, focusing on the relationship and communication aspect of PR. Even though he did not manage to publish his life-long project about Greek PR (Yoel, personal communication), Pavlidis published a book in 2000. Pavlidis' book, entitled *Cultural Communication*, demonstrated the importance he placed on communication elements which the term 'Dimosies Sxeseis' did not accurately express. The field of practice of this early practitioner generation was to make the market aware of PR, how it worked and to create external awareness that PR was practiced in Greece.

Between 1980, when HPRA opened membership, and end of the 1990s, even though the need to emphasize on PR strategy is evident, the focus was more on the professional practice of PR with a narrower and more specific meaning of the concept. Coutoupis' *Practical Guide for PR* and Magnisalis' *Public Relations: Theory and Techniques of Relationship*

DOI: 10.1057/9781137427519.0009

with the Public reflected the need of the practitioners to be more involved deeper with PR and learn more about the practice of the discipline. Even though Magnisalis wrote the first edition in 1970 and the tenth in 2002, his book had a major impact during both decades in-between as it offered invaluable insight of the profession's trends. According to Grunig et al. (1995), when attempting to cluster PR practice in Greece, it seems that PR practitioners undertook activities which were under the 'press agentry' model or to an extent the 'public information' model.

After the mid-1990s, Lavetzis identifies additional interest in areas such as crisis communication management, corporate communication, financial PR, internal PR and CSR (Papatriantafyllou, 2008). The major textbooks used by Athens University of Economics and Business, the most prestigious higher education institution of the country in the field of business studies, were written by Panigyrakis and Ventoura (2001) and Papalexandris (2001). Both books cover contemporary PR aspects, such as crisis management, sponsorship and online PR, thus complementing existing topics such as the evaluation and management of PR programmes.

The 2013 census published by EDEE provides numerical evidence concerning the industry of advertising, promotional and one-to-one marketing, PR and the industry of media specialists, which, surprisingly, is not considered part of PR. Focusing only on PR (Table 1) the consequences of the Greek economic crisis are evident when examining 'turnover', 'gross income' and 'number of employees'.

TABLE 1   *EDEE Census for PR 2006–2013*

Item \ Year	2006	2007	2008	2009	2010	2011	2012	2013
No of agencies	–	–	20	–	–	20	–	18
Turnover (mil. €)	35,876	44,690	54,710	65,221	37,574	41,411	34,228	–
Gross income (mil. €)	15,025	19,203	22,771	22,448	13,836	13,475	11,471	–
No of employees	270	–	380	–	308–		295	–
Men (%)	–	–	25	–	28–		33	–
Women (%)	–	–	75	–	72–		67	–
Education								
High School	–	–	14	–	14–		4	–
Bachelor's	–	–	54	–	54–		61	–
Postgraduate	–	–	32	–	32–		35	–

Source: Table developed for needs of this study. Summary of EDEE Census 2009, 2011, 2013 (http://www.edee.gr/default.asp?pid=26&la=1).

DOI: 10.1057/9781137427519.0009

A notable result of the economic crisis is that employing agencies can now 'afford' better-educated personnel, which has other societal consequences, and that the percentage of men in PR agency employment rose from 25 to 33 per cent in five years.

Discussion

A more radical development of PR might have been expected after such a promising start in 1951. Even so, PR in Greece has been developing over the previous 60 years and, given that the country has been experiencing financial difficulties after 1999 and is suffering a financial crisis since 2010, the consequences for the PR industry could have been much worse.

Coutoupis (personal communication) identified a number of obstacles that prevented the field from blooming. These points have been raised occasionally in Greek books and some were also mentioned by interviewees.

The topics are inter-correlated. Each issue is, or could be, the reason triggering another issue and vice versa:

a. International influences had a major impact on how PR has been practiced. These influences also affected practitioners and academics when adopting and developing a definition of PR. That there is no single definition of PR may be perceived as a global debate; however, this issue supports the point made by the pioneers back in the pre-1980s period that the specific translation given to PR in Greek (Dimosies Sxeseis) does not reflect accurately what PR is. The 'paradox' of this point is that Greek practitioners and academics have attempted to provide over the years with definitions of what PR is, without agreeing on a single definition.

b. The Greek PR industry did not manage to draw successfully borderlines separating the discipline and its functions from marketing and advertising. Clients continue to request that PR consultants and agencies engage with marketing and advertising activities. Coutoupis (personal communication) quoted a response from HPRA research conducted in 1999 saying that 37 per cent of clients expect to raise the sales. This lack of understanding coming from clients and, in cases, a lack of understanding by practitioners

DOI: 10.1057/9781137427519.0009

have not allowed PR to colonize areas such as sponsorship, CSR, and political communication and has led to the false perception that these practices belong to the marketing sphere.

c. Even though PR practitioners were amongst those who adopted the IPRA Code of Athens, thus sharing Matrat's vision, and the PR sector of EDEE signed up to the more recent Stockholm Charter, Coutoupis' was one of the first calls for mechanisms to ensure that deontological codes of practice and ethics are followed within the country. These codes are given lip service but not enforced.

d. Finally, the most important issue has been the lack of education for the field of PR. Yannas (2004) reports that PR was taught as part of a broader curriculum in Athens University of Economics and Business, University of Macedonia and business departments of Technological Educational Institutions (TEI) since the mid-1980s (p. 173) and by Panteion University, University of Athens and University of Thessaloniki in the 1990s. None of these programmes awards a degree in PR. The first programme which awarded a degree in PR was founded in Kastoria in 1999 (TEI Kozanis, under the supervision of Yannas). The Department of Public Relations and Communication there, however, was revalidated in 2013 but retitled as the Department of Digital Media and Communication (2013). In 2003 the second Department of Public Relations and Communication was founded in Argostoli (TEI Ionian Islands) in 2003 which was again revalidated as a Department of Digital Media and Communication ten years later. Both programmes had relatively low entry criteria before revalidation. Coutoupis (1992) also identified the lack of PR education highlighting that it was taught within the framework of seminars or specific private colleges and universities.

Conclusions

The historic development of Greek PR has a number of peculiarities. The start was impressive and promising. The state showed genuine interest and took the initiative (following US advice) by attempting to enhance Greek tourism through PR and by practicing PR at the Public Power Corporation SA (one of the largest public organizations). International

DOI: 10.1057/9781137427519.0009

agencies and multinational organizations with in-house PR offered extensive 'know-how' to local employees, while Greek private companies started seeing the value of PR and hired PR practitioners. A team of 20–25 self-motivated and highly educated individuals led the way by researching and practicing PR at a national level, while a handful of these pioneers also played a very significant role representing the country internationally through IPRA.

In the 1980s and 1990s, Greece experienced great change by becoming member of EEC/EU. Among other benefits, the EEC/EU membership led to a boom in the services sector and inward tourism. The overall change of the market provided new opportunities for individuals to find jobs at entry level or middle-management level in professions where vocational studies were adequate. This led to a rapid expansion of the PR profession mainly in non-managerial roles. Two of the positive outcomes of this era were: that PR started having substance even though clients still could not always see the differences with marketing and advertising; and the developments that occurred in higher education with the founding of PR programmes and the teaching of PR as part of a communication curriculum.

The post-2000 era could have been seen as an era of PR maturity with professional practice and academia attempting to approach each other through initiatives such as IoC; however, the financial instability has had rapid negative consequences for both areas.

PR in Greece has always been influenced by the US, British and French schools of thought although significant cultural differences make it the amalgam it is today. The framing of PR under a managerial umbrella has been widely adopted by Greek PR practitioners; however, it becomes evident from Greek PR literature and interviews that PR is strongly linked with social issues and causes. These views follow the French and British schools of thought but also rely on Greek inner beliefs for social justice and dialogue. Communication of matters with cultural importance, political communication and the role of PR as an ethical advocate are placed high on the agenda of those Greek PR practitioners and academics who have demonstrated over the years an in-depth understanding for the discipline.

Note: The author thanks Greek PR pioneers Thalis Coutoupis, Rita Malikouti, Andrew C. Rizopoulos and the late Marcel Yoel for their time and insights.

DOI: 10.1057/9781137427519.0009

References

Bini, E., Fasce, F. and Muzi Falconi, T. (2011) 'The Origins and Early Developments of Public Relations in Italy, 1945–1960', *Journal of Communication Management*, 15(3), 210–222.

Bokovou, P. (1974) *Η λειτουργία των δημοσίων σχέσεων εις την σύγχρονον οικονομίαν* [Public Relations Function in Modern Economy] (Self-Published: Thessaloniki, Greece).

Coutoupis, T. (1992) *Πρακτικός Οδηγός Δημοσίων Σχέσεων* [Practical Guide to Public Relations], 3rd edition (Athens, Greece: Galeos).

Department of Digital Media and Communication (2013) Technological Education Institute of Western Macedonia. *History*, http://kastoria.teikoz.gr/pr/html_eng/wrap.php?file=/contents/geninfo/history.htm, date accessed 16 August 2014.

Grunig, J., Dozier, D., Ehling, W., Grunig, L., Repper, F. and White, J. (1992) *Excellence in Public Relations and Communication Management* (Mahwah, NJ: Lawrence Erlbaum Associates).

Grunig, J., Grunig, L., Sriramesh, K., Huang, Y. and Lyra, A. (1995) 'Models of Public Relations in an International Setting', *Journal of Public Relations Research*, 7(3), 163–186.

Hellenic Association of Advertising and Communication Agencies (2011) *Διαφήμιση και επικοινωνία σε αριθμούς* [Advertising and Communication in Numbers], http://www.edee.gr/files/Cencus/Final_EDEE_Census%202011.pdf , date accessed 05 August 2014.

Hellenic Association of Advertising and Communication Agencies (2014), *Ιστορία* [History], http://www.edee.gr/default.asp?pid=23&la=1, date accessed 05 August 2014.

IoC – Institute of Communication (Producer) (2003) *Interview with Manos Pavlidis* [Undated, Audio Recording] (Athens, Greece).

IoC – Institute of Communication (Producer) (2004) *Interview with Marcel Yoel* [Undated, Audio Recording] (Athens, Greece).

IPRA (1960) *Minutes of the Seventh Meeting of the Council of the International Public Relations Association*, 26 April 1960 (Holland: The Hague).

Magkliveras, D. (1965) *Οι Δημόσιες Σχέσεις στο Κράτος* [Public Relations in the State] (Kallithea, Greece: Greek Centre of Productivity).

Magkliveras, D. (1970) *Στοιχεία Δημοσίων Σχέσεων – Θεωρία και πράξις* [Elements of Public Relations – Theory and Practice], 3rd edition (Athens, Greece: Graphic Arts E. Valasakis Ltd).

DOI: 10.1057/9781137427519.0009

Magnisalis, K., (2002) Δημόσιες Σχέσεις.Θεωρία και Τεχνική των Σχέσεων με το Κοινό [Public Relations. Theory and Technique of Relationships with the Public], 10th edition (Athens, Greece: Interbooks).

Panigyrakis, G., and Ventoura, Z. (2001) Σύγχρονη διοικητική δημοσίων σχέσεων [Contemporary Management of Public Relations] (Athens, Greece: G. Benou).

Papalexandris, N. (2001) Δημόσιες σχέσεις – η λειτουργία της επικοινωνίας στη σύγχρονη επιχείρηση [Public Relations – The Function of Communication in Modern Business] (Athens, Greece: G. Benou).

Papamichalakis, I. (1961) Αί Δημόσιαι και ανθρώπιναι σχέσεις εις τας συγχρόνους τράπεζα και οικονομικούς οργανισμούς (public and human relations) – η εφαρμογή παρά των τραπεζών και οικονομικών οργανισμών εν Ελλάδι [Public and Human Relations in Modern Banks and Economic Organizations (Public and Human Relations – Function in Banks and Economic Organizations in Greece] (Athens, Greece: DIFROS).

Papamichalakis, I. (1970) Γενική Εισαγωγή εις τας δημόσιας σχέσεις [General Introduction to Public Relations] (Athens, Greece: Klapakis).

Papatriantafyllou, G. (2008) Προγράμματα δημοσίων σχέσεων – στρατηγική & εκτέλεση [Public Relations Programmes – Strategy & Execution] (Athens, Greece: A. Stamoulis).

Pavlidis, M. (2000) Πολιτισμική Επικοινωνία [Cultural Communication] (Athens, Greece: Exantas).

Rodríguez-Salcedo, N. (2008) 'Public Relations before "Public Relations" in Spain: An Early History (1881–1960)', Journal of Communication Management, 12(4), 279–293.

Theofilou, A. and Watson, T. (2014) 'The History of Public Relations in Greece from 1950 to 1980: Professionalization of the "Art"', Public Relations Review, 40(4), 700–706.

Tsiligiannis, K. (1973) Δημόσιαι Σχέσεις και Αθρωπολογία – Η Συμβολή της πολιτισμικής, της κοινωνικής και της εφηρμοσμένης ανθρωπολογίας επι των Δημοσίων Σχέσεων [Public Relations and Anthropology – The Contribution of Cultural, Social and Applied Anthropology on Public Relations] (Thessaloniki, Greece: Papageorgiou).

Watson, T. (2011) 'Archive of the International Public Relations Association', Bournemouth University, http://microsites. bournemouth.ac.uk/historyofpr/ipra-archive/, date accessed 05 August 2014.

DOI: 10.1057/9781137427519.0009

Yannas, P. (2004) 'Greece', in B. van Ruler and D. Verčič (eds), *Public Relations and Communication Management in Europe: A Nation-by-Nation Introduction to Public Relations Theory and* Practice (Berlin: Mouton de Gruyter).

Zobanakis, S. (1965) *Συμβολή εις την ιστορίαν των Δημοσίων Σχέσεων* [Contribution to Public Relations History] (Athens, Greece: Graphic Arts I. Makris).

Zobanakis, S. (1974) *Δημοσιαι Σχέσεις* [Public Relations], 2nd edition (Athens, Greece: Klapakis).

DOI: 10.1057/9781137427519.0009

6
Italy

Toni Muzi Falconi and Fabio Ventoruzzo

Abstract: *From the end of World War II to the fall of the Berlin Wall in 1989, Italians lived in a 'blocked political democratic system' (Ginsburg, 2001; Jones, 2003).*

This is the political and cultural humus in which Public Relations (PR) activities have developed: a continued communication effort to deter a Communist seizure of national power. A strong underlying influence that characterized the profession was the Anglo-American 'communicating-to' matrix approach in which propaganda and persuasion are the main purpose (Muzi Falconi, 2005). The profession consolidated during the post-war reconstruction (1945–1955), the economic miracle (1955–1965), the socio-economic slowdown (1965/1975) and stagnation (1975–1990). Following almost a decade (1992–2000) of 'wound-licking' induced by a corruption scandal of the early 1990s, the institutionalization of PR and a transition to the communicating-with approach characterized the first decade (2000–2010) of this new century.

Keywords: cronyism; institutionalization; internationalization; masters of ceremony; PR infrastructure; society

Watson, Tom (ed.). *Western European Perspectives on the Development of Public Relations: Other Voices*. Basingstoke: Palgrave Macmillan, 2015. DOI: 10.1057/9781137427519.0010.

Italy is a relatively young nation state: united as a monarchy in 1861 and a parliamentary democracy since 1946. Acclaimed as hosting the world's largest cultural heritage, Italy in Western Europe counts the lowest percentage per inhabitants of university graduates, as well as of book and newspaper readers. With almost 60 million citizens, Italy hosts one of the oldest populations in the world in terms of average age, as well as an elite that sociologists estimate as fewer than 10,000, in the absence of any decent social mobility.

In this 'cronItaly' (Muzi Falconi, 2009), rooted on relationships aimed to preserve the status quo, the evolution of the profession has mostly interpreted the role of 'master of ceremony' to the country's highly segmented leaderships (ibid.). Social critics increasingly accuse public relations (PR) of advocating almost exclusively on behalf of strong and powerful interests. On the other hand, this 'master of ceremonies' role to support leaderships is coherent with the traditional stereotype that, across the diverse roles a professional performs in, or for, the organization, a core expertise lies in facilitating smooth relationships between the major segments of leadership: political, economic, cultural, media and social systems (Muzi Falconi, 2009).

According to industry estimates, there are some 110,000 individuals in Italy who invest more than 50 per cent of their professional time in programmed relationship-building activities with stakeholders and publics for social, private- and public-sector organizations.

In 1994, only 22 per cent of the 300 largest Italian companies had a dedicated division or department for PR/external relations (Invernizzi and Romenti, 2009). By 2013, this had risen to 84 per cent, according to IULM University and Ketchum (Prima Online, 2014). Some 42.4 per cent are permanent members of executive boards and another 24.9 per cent are regularly invited to participate in board activities (for a total of 67.5 per cent). The consolidation of the PR profession has, however, been challenged in recent years by economic and social transition from decline and stagnation to an enduring recession and deflation.

When it started

Documented antecedents may be traced back to 1934 (Bini, Fasce and Muzi Falconi, 2010) when Linoleum, the floor tile company belonging to the Pirelli group, opened its first formally titled PR department, and to

DOI: 10.1057/9781137427519.0010

1936 when Mussolini, preoccupied that the US would eventually join the UK in actively trying to stop the Italian dictator's planned invasion of Ethiopia, sent Bernardo Bergamaschi from the government's Propaganda Office to collect funds from the always powerful and rich Italian migrant communities and, with that money, lobbied Washington in a successful attempt to avert such a turn of events (Colarizi, 2000). Thus US-style PR arrived in Sicily in 1943 and was consolidated when the Marshall Plan was implemented in 1947 (Muzi Falconi, 2005).

The first country to abandon the Axis in 1943, Italy was an experimental ground for the Allies to identify the more effective ways to re-establish quality relationships with local communities following the violent occupation of Italy (Colarizi, 2000). Thus the Allied Command recruited in the US, and moved civilian PR operators of Italian origins to Sicily, some of whom were also members of the Mafia, and left them behind to administer the occupied areas of Sicily to counter fears that local power might shift to the Communist Party, while the troops proceeded to the liberation of the rest of the country from the Nazis and Fascists (Bini, Fasce and Muzi Falconi, 2010).

With the first post-war political elections of 1948, the activities of the USIS (United States Information Service), already secretly active in Italy since 1943, became public and by deploying many channels, tools and activities succeeded in helping the DC defeat the challenge of the Communist Party (Muzi Falconi, 2005). Amongst the major PR-related factors contributing to this result were a USIS-led letter-writing campaign by Italian immigrants in the US to relatives in Italy urging them to vote for the Catholic DC party, and an impressive campaign, supported with substantial financial resources, led by Vanni Montana, an American trade unionist, to disrupt the Socialist–Communist parties axis by inducing a split in the former (ibid.).

The development of the Cold War led USIS to undertake intense activity of exchanges and visits amongst Italian business, student, academic, social and economic elites, which were mostly interested in developing and exchanging scientific, technological, sociological and communication knowledge (Colarizi, 2007). Also, Italy's strategic position in the centre of the Mediterranean induced USIS to step up its activities to improve relationships with Italians by attracting them with films, brochures, papers and leaflets to the 'mirage' and principles of the 'American dream' (Muzi Falconi, 2005). Many Italians were also recruited by the USIS and employed in PR activities (Bini, Fasce and Muzi Falconi, 2010) and this

DOI: 10.1057/9781137427519.0010

became the initial training base of the country's first professionals (e.g. Alvise Barison and Guido De Rossi del Nero, who both remained active for decades that followed).

Three urban centres hosted the growth of the profession during the reconstruction effort until the mid-1960s (Bini, Fasce and Muzi Falconi, 2010): Genoa (hub of the multinational oil companies such as Standard Oil, Mobil and Shell, and Italsider, the state-owned steel manufacturer); Rome (hub of the USIS, the government and the nascent political parties and institutions); and Milan (the financial and business centre).

The role of these new PR officers was fundamental in developing networks of communication and information. They implemented planned efforts to explain their employers' activities, projects and results, mostly by using the printed media and the radio. They also acted as the 'eyes and ears' of their employers (and not just their 'voices') by capturing, interpreting the expectations and needs of local communities and reporting these to their management and therefore disseminating relevant news, information and corporate policies.

In 1952, Roberto Tremelloni, a moderate pro-American social democrat who later became Finance Minister, opened the 'Instituto per le Relazioni Pubbliche' (IPR), an association formed by scholars and managers with the aim of disseminating the principles and practices of PR. Publications, radio programmes, professional development seminars and conferences were its core activities (Muzi Falconi, 2005). In 1954, IPR also launched the first Oscar di Bilancio, a company annual report award that today (managed by FERPI, Italian federation of public relations professionals) remains the most reputed and most sought-after award in the country (Scarpulla, 2008). Ironically, the first company to receive this Oscar in 1954 was Motta (Italian bakery and cakes) whose annual report was for the first time included with its annual financial results.

The birth of Italy's PR culture

Olivetti, the typewriter company, under the charismatic leadership of its owner–intellectual Adriano Olivetti, undertook visionary local and global PR practices. Many young architects, writers, designers, poets and philosophers were attracted by Olivetti to become PR operators in the broadest interpretation, including employee and corporate communication, corporate social responsibility (CSR) and stakeholder relations,

DOI: 10.1057/9781137427519.0010

marketing and visual communication, as well as public affairs (Bini, Fasce and Muzi Falconi, 2010). The Olivetti organization, even after its owner's death in 1960, exemplified Italy's best PR practice well into the 1970s.

Another remarkable experience in those years was that of IRI Group (Instituto Ricostruzione Industriale), a huge conglomerate of State-owned manufacturing companies, where a like-minded group of Catholic CEOs succeeded in creating dialogue with hard-line Communist trade unionists (Fasce, 2000) by deploying effective and creative 'inclusive' employee and community two-way relationship programmes to support and sustain the dramatic economic upturn of the economy from the 1950s to the mid-1960s.

ENI (Ente Nazionale Idrocarburi), the national oil company under the leadership of Enrico Mattei, decided to challenge the 'seven sisters' (major oil companies) in the Mediterranean and North Africa. By employing some of the most respected journalists and intellectuals as PR professionals, it implemented a highly unconventional public diplomacy programme that succeeded in opening economic cooperation and trade with many Arab and Soviet bloc countries (Bini, Fasce and Muzi Falconi, 2010).

Even Edison, the private electricity monopoly, influenced by the worldwide success of film-maker Robert Flaherty's 'Louisiana Story' documentary from Standard Oil, decided to also embark on documentary production and recruited the well-known director Ermanno Olmi (Muzi Falconi, 2005). This activity was continued after 1963 by Enel, when Edison was nationalized and renamed.

Other companies active in PR activities in the late 1950s were Pirelli, with a programme that disseminated modern management practices to the private sector through publications, workshops and seminars (Bini, Fasce and Muzi Falconi, 2010), and the film manufacturer Ferrania, acquired in 1964 by the US-owned 3M Company and which, until the early 1970s, ran an intense PR programme to support young Italian photographers and researchers while developing an archive of historic and contemporary photography.

From many perspectives, the social policies of Italian companies, with Olivetti and ENI first in line, as well as their communication activities with employees and local communities, became a benchmark model for many other European countries (Valentini, 2009). For example, the German corporate governance practice of 'mitbestimmung' (trade union representatives elected as board members) was inspired by Italy's reconstruction period, as were the UK's Confederation of British Industry best practices in internal communication.

In 1956, the first European Congress of Public Relations with major European business and political leaders as active participants was staged by Lake Stresa: papers and discussions indicated a trend towards integrating public and human relations along the lines of the moderate Catholic/trade union coalition of interests (Muzi Falconi, 2005).

The (troubled) dialogue with society

In 1961 in Rome, Father Felix Morlion, a Jesuit well-known for ties with both Opus Dei and the CIA and much interest in PR, launched the first Master's programme in PR at the ProDeo International Social Sciences University (Mainini, 2002). In those years, businesses relied on intellectuals, often social democrats or socialists, for their PR activities in an attempt to bridge the socio-cultural gap between civil society and corporate elites (ibid.). With the advent of the first Centre–Left government in 1963, businesses needed to reinvigorate their dialogue with the political system. Earlier, their relationship with the country's Left had been mostly focused on trade union relationships and was left to the personnel departments, while the political dialogue with the Catholic DC party and other, smaller coalition parties was dealt with directly by entrepreneurs or by their PR advisers (Muzi Falconi, 2012).

Using a planned PR programme, Antonio Giolitti (Socialist Budget Minister) and his assistant Giorgio Ruffolo created the narratives for economic planning; to attract private investment to the South of Italy, they proposed 'programmed negotiation': an attempt to direct investments to underdeveloped areas with ad hoc negotiated incentives (Bini, Fasce and Muzi Falconi, 2010).

In 1964, trade unions, following weeks of strikes, negotiated a 'due information agreement' with the automobile industry: trade unions needed to be informed in advance of any new management decision and decided when and how to inform the workers. This 'pyrrhic' victory was a huge backward step for employee communication. This agreement stayed in place until 1982 when the 'march of the 40,000' in Torino, led by Fiat's CEO Cesare Romiti, resulted in management to re-appropriating the right to dialogue with employees (Muzi Falconi, 2005).

DOI: 10.1057/9781137427519.0010

From the end of the 1960s the political system became paralyzed and social tension increased, first with the birth of the student movement and then with the awakening of the labour movement (Colarizi, 2007). Disconnected from the public and with the complicity of a media system owned by powerful economic forces, government parties and the business community, covered by the dust of flamboyant PR activities, indulged in increasingly opaque corruption and dialogue with society (Muzi Falconi, 2005).

The Italian Federation of Public Relations (FERPI) was created in 1970 through the merger of two existing associations, both formed in 1956. Rome-based FIRP represented the community of professionals tied to the public sector, large state-owned corporations and public affairs consultants; while FIERPI (based in Milan) reflected the community of professionals employed in the private and financial sectors and the few, at the time, agencies and media relations consultants (Muzi Falconi, 2005). From its inception, FERPI was committed to advocate the value of PR profession; its activities were inspired by liberal and progressive leaderships that supported the country's quest for modernization and development by launching many cultural stimuli to its members: from the rise of the consumer protection wave; the quest for citizen participation; the formation of public policy; the adoption of IPRA Code of Athens ethics and the net refusal to accept a state-controlled corporative guild structure, but rather to align with EU liberals' demand for a free and open exchange of all professional practices (Scarpulla, 2008).

The second part of the 1970s was characterized by the 'austerity' interpretation of social progress invoked by Enrico Berlinguer, the Communist Party leader; the anti-private business culture of the RAI television monopoly; and the explosion of terrorist activities (Colarizi, 2007). All these variables created vast operational business and political spaces for the two Milanese 'friends' Bettino Craxi and Silvio Berlusconi, a relationship which would hugely expand in the following decade (Muzi Falconi, 2011).

The role of the image culture

In the 1980s, with the complicity of the 'modern' culture of a Socialist Party, whose strength was more and more disproportionate vis-à-vis its tiny electoral weight, and the continued pre-industrial and pauperistic

DOI: 10.1057/9781137427519.0010

culture of the two major parties (Catholic and Communist), Berlusconi's and Craxi's 'image culture' (today the term would be 'visibility') triumphed (Muzi Falconi, 2011). This 'image culture' was characterized by persistent and persuasive communication (ibid., 2005).

In 1981, six of the country's major PR firms gave birth to Assorel, the association of agencies. Not in competition with FERPI, Assorel recognized the former as the representative of the profession and promoted internal (contractual criteria and guidelines to the value of an agency vis-à-vis solo consultants) and external promotional activities for the service side of the profession (Scarpulla, 2008).

In 1985, Luca di Montezemolo, who later became President of Fiat and then Ferrari, left his powerful PR directorship at Fiat and created Azzurra, a consortium of Italian companies that participated with great fanfare but little success in yacht racing, America's Cup, a first example of a consortium built around a PR programme (Muzi Falconi, 2005).

These are also the years of the international success of Italian fashion: Beppe Modenese, a highly reputed PR professional active since the early 1960s (initially on behalf of DuPont), played a primary role and became the first global 'guru' of fashion PR.

Major Italian companies, such as Alitalia, Ferruzzi and Montedison, redesigned their 'image' and invested heavily in advice from Landor Associates, the-then famous corporate identity designers from San Francisco. For the first time, in the second half of the 1980s, businesses invested more to learn what consumers thought about their communication than about their products (Bini, Fasce and Muzi Falconi, 2010).

In 1986, immediately following the Chernobyl nuclear explosion in Ukraine, Rome hosted the second European Congress of Public Relations with the title 'Public Relations in a Changing European Society' where the principal issues discussed were consumer and environmental protection (Scarpulla, 2008).

Between 1984 and 1987 SCR, Italy's leading PR agency, acquired by Shandwick in 1989, made a considerable effort to rationalize and disseminate a practice-based descriptive approach to PR called 'Gorel' (Governance of Relationships) that also introduced a methodology to effectively measure the results of PR programme. Fifteen years later in 2002, the first edition of a book on 'Gorel' authored by FERPI President Toni Muzi Falconi was published. A second edition was published in 2005.

DOI: 10.1057/9781137427519.0010

Also, in the second part of the 1980s, Italian practice adopted and adapted a perverse national corruption cycle between business, political and media systems that in 1992 will lead to 'Mani Pulite' (Clean Hands), the scandal that dismantled all the political parties that had formed the first Republic in 1947 (Muzi Falconi, 2005; Bini, Fasce and Muzi Falconi, 2010).

Institutionalization of the profession

The Mani Pulite scandal involved a considerable number of PR professionals accused by the prosecutors of intermediating and promoting unlawful operations between businesses, political parties and the media (Muzi Falconi, 2012). As a counter move, a campaign for the privatization of state-owned companies was launched in 1993 by a transitional government headed by Carlo Azeglio Ciampi, the future President of the Republic, with his PR adviser Paolo Peluffo, as well as his-then economic adviser and (2014) Governor of the European Central Bank, Mario Draghi. They proposed the UK privatization schema as a blueprint for the Italian market in which PR advisers led all communication efforts (Bini, Fasce and Muzi Falconi, 2010). This unexpected move gave energy to Italy's PR practice and helped it recover from the Mani Pulite scandal.

In the 1994 elections, Silvio Berlusconi surprised all with a massive 'viral' campaign based on thousands of 'multipliers' scattered in every corner of the country. Many were recruited from his commercial advertising sales force and his clients, mostly composed of small business owners (Muzi Falconi, 2012). Also with the help of a huge campaign of mega posters, he was elected Prime Minister. Two years later, in elections following the collapse of the Berlusconi coalition, Romano Prodi, supported by his PR adviser Silvio Sircana, became Prime Minister. However, he was, in turn, replaced two years later, in 1998, by Communist Party member Massimo D'Alema, assisted by PR professionals Claudio Velardi (today a lobbyist) and Gianni Cuperlo (today a politician himself). Thus there were three Prime Ministers in six years who based their success on persuasive communication and their failures on the inability to deliver what they had promised with their PR activities.

From 1997, major corporations again became involved in intense communication activities, and the quality of demand greatly improved in its professional competence with the entry into organizations of many senior professionals (Muzi Falconi, 2005).

DOI: 10.1057/9781137427519.0010

The election in 1999 of Carlo Azeglio Ciampi to the Presidency of the Republic, accompanied by his spokesperson Paolo Peluffo, initiated seven years (until 2006) of an ongoing and effectively planned PR programme to strengthen the sense of belonging of Italians to the Nation in the wider context of the principles of the European Union. This election also led to the appointment of a formal 'PR Adviser' for the first time to the President's office, Arrigo Levi, a reputed journalist and former editor of TG1, the most popular Italian TV news programme. With the election of Romano Prodi as President of the European Union in 2001, a new position of manager of communication of the Commission (not simply the spokesperson) was formed in Brussels with former economic journalist Ricardo Franco Levi as director.

Since 2000, corporate communication and PR practices in Italy have taken another quantum leap. Law 150/2000 recognized the strategic role of communication in public-sector organizations (Muzi Falconi, 2005) and made it mandatory for public administration offices to establish three distinct functions: relationships with publics, spokesperson for the political leadership and media relations. Unfortunately, the latter function was officially limited to professional journalists who belonged to a specific and then-powerful guild.

On the social/non-profit front, the active presence of personalities such as Susanna Agnelli, Umberto Veronesi, Giovanni Moro; the experience of the dedicated newsweekly *Vita* edited by Riccardo Bonacina; and forward-looking associations such as the CSR and sustainability foundation Sodalitas, as well as excellent PR practitioners, including Giangi Milesi from Cevsi, Carlo Barburini from the Meyer Paediatric Hospital and Alessandra Veronese from the Eye Bank in Venice have given dignity and quality to the reputation of Italy's non-profit PR.

On the business and private enterprise front, PR's role has risen in organizational charts and the professional areas of expertise have shifted from traditional media relations/lobbying activities to a more integrated mix (ibid.).

Ludovico Passerin d'Entreves (Fiat), Gianluca Comin and Paolo Iammatteo (Enel), Carlo Fornaro (Vodafone and then Telecom Italia), Andrea Prandi (Indesit and then Edison), Stefano Lucchini (ENI) and Anna Adriani (illycaffè) have all been recognized as practice leaders of the Italian PR community.

The public relations consulting and agency sector continues to consolidate its presence: the Italian Barabino & Partners today is the largest

DOI: 10.1057/9781137427519.0010

while other international firms have consolidated their presence since the inception of Assorel.

In the late 1900s and 2000s, Italian university education in PR became more systematically organized (Muzi Falconi and Kodilja, 2004). Besides IULM University in Milan (still the leading university for PR education) PR degree courses were set up in the Universities of Udine (northern Italy) and Catania (southern Italy) as well. Many communication science programmes hosting PR courses were introduced in other universities (ibid.). In 2003, FERPI and Assorel formed Consulta Education, a special project with a proactive role in defining and evaluating the university courses in PR and Communication Management (Scarpulla, 2008). A special 'endorsement' was granted to university courses whose curricula were coherent with the competences required by the PR profession.

All through the first decade of the new century FERPI, under various leaderships, has been very active in advocating the value of PR with stakeholders (external as well as its own members) in order to avoid the misperception/misunderstanding of its role, and to maintain a strong and visible distance from many scandals and irresponsible behaviours (both personal and organizational) that populated the media and political agendas during those years (Muzi Falconi, 2005).

In the international arena, FERPI was one of the founding members of the Global Alliance for Public Relations and Communication Management (GA), and in 2003 under the presidency of the Italian founding chair of the new global organizations, the first World PR Festival was held in Rome which attracted more than 400 delegates from 27 nations and led to the signing of a new GA global ethics protocol (Muzi Falconi, 2005).

In this international awakening, FERPI members not only networked with their colleagues from all over the world, but also voiced their studies and practices in all of these forums. Italy was evident as a leading international player by representing, besides the founding chairmanship of GA (Toni Muzi Falconi), its general secretariat (Amanda Succi) and Board (Biagio Oppi). It also facilitated an Italian scholar (Emanuele Invernizzi) in becoming President of the European Public Relations Education and Research Association (EUPRERA) that held its 2008 Congress in Milan on the theme of the institutionalization of the PR function in organizations.

DOI: 10.1057/9781137427519.0010

Conclusion

At the heart of Italian PR, four characteristics of the evolution of PR's impact in Italy stand out:

1   Its infrastructure is characterized by intense interdependence and interrelationships among the leaderships (often overlapping) of political, economic and media elites (Muzi Falconi, 2009). This may be found in other countries, but the critical overview and 'watchdog' roles on PR activities that exist in other countries (e.g. PR Watch in the US and Spinwatch in the UK) are missing in Italy as media is mostly owned and influenced by businesses who also determine the fate of political parties (Muzi Falconi, 2009; Bini, Fasce and Muzi Falconi, 2010).

2   Since the dissemination of the Bled Manifesto (van Ruler and Verčič, 2002) Italy's more-aware PR community had differentiated from the traditional Anglo-American model; this has encouraged the development of an Italian body of knowledge (Muzi Falconi and Kodilja, 2004).

3   The impact of the 2002 Bled Manifesto also accelerated the international quest for generic principles and specific applications knowledge base (Muzi Falconi, 2009) that allowed Italian professionals and scholars to play a central role in the development of the Global Alliance for Public Relations and Communication Management.

4   The acknowledgement that PR is either global in its approach or is not (ibid.) constitutes a distributed professional capital that has allowed many senior Italian professionals to introduce daring and innovative practices in major companies with global perspectives, including Enel, ENI and Luxottica.

References

Bini, E., Fasce, F. and Muzi Falconi, T. (2010) *The Origins and Early Developments of Public Relations in Italy, 1945–1960*, Paper presented at the International History of Public Relations Conference, Bournemouth, UK, 8–9 July 2010, http://microsites.bournemouth.ac.uk/historyofpr/files/2010/11/IHPRC-2010-Proceedings.pdf, date accessed 27 October 2014.

DOI: 10.1057/9781137427519.0010

Colarizi, S. (2000) *L'opinione degli italiani sotto il regime 1929–1943* [The Opinion of Italians during the Regime 1945–1960] (Bari: Laterza).

Colarizi, S. (2007) Storia politica della Repubblica [Political History of the Italian Republic 1943–2006] (Bari: Laterza).

Fasce, F. (2000) *La democrazia degli affari. Comunicazione aziendale e discorso pubblico negli Stati Uniti, 1900–1940* [The Democracy of Business. Corporate Communication and Public Discourse in the Unites States, 1900–1940] (Rome: Carocci).

Ginsburg, P. (2001) *Italy and Its Discontents* (London: Penguin).

Invernizzi, E. and Romenti, S. (2009) 'Strategic Communication and Decision-Making Processes: Toward the Communication Oriented Organisation', *academicus*, http://www.academicus.edu.al/nr3/ Academicus-MMXI-3-012-027.pdf, date accessed 10 November 2014.

Jones, T. (2003). *The Dark Side of Italy* (New York: North Point Press).

Mainini, V. (2002) 'Storia delle Relazioni Pubbliche Italiane dal 1946 al 1970' [History of Italian PR 1946–1970], unpublished Master's thesis (IULM University, Milan, Italy).

Muzi Falconi, T. (2005) *Governare le Relazioni* [The Relationships Government] (Milano: IlSole24Ore).

Muzi Falconi, T. (2009) 'Public Relations in Italy: Master of Ceremonies in a Relational Society', in K. Sriramesh and D. Verčič (eds) *The Global Public Relations Handbook: Theory, Research, and Practice*, Revised edition (New York: Routledge).

Muzi Falconi, T. (2012) 'The Rise and Fall of Berlusconi's Cuckoo Model of Public Relations 1992–2011', Paper presented at the International History of Public Relations Conference, Bournemouth, UK, 11–12 July 2013, http://microsites.bournemouth.ac.uk/historyofpr/ files/2010/11/IHPRC-2012-Proceedings2.pdf, date accessed 27 October 2014.

Muzi Falconi, T. (2013) 'The 1982 collapse of Banco Ambrosiano: Critiquing professional memoirs towards a reliable history of PR', Paper presented at the International History of Public Relations Conference, Bournemouth, UK, 25–26 June 2013, http://microsites. bournemouth.ac.uk/historyofpr/files/2010/11/IHPRC-2013- Proceedings-Revised.pdf, date accessed 27 October 2014.

Muzi Falconi, T. and Kodilja, R. (2004) 'Italy', in B. van Ruler and D. Verčič (eds) *Public Relations and Communication Management in Europe: A Nation-By-Nation Introduction to Public Relations Theory and Practice* (Berlin: Mouton De Gruyter).

DOI: 10.1057/9781137427519.0010

Prima Online (2014) 'Osservatorio Iulm-Ketchum: misurazione della reputazione, un asset strategico per l'impresa' [IULM-Ketchum Observatory: Of Reputation; Reputation Measurment, a Strategic Business Asset], 9 June 2014, http://www.primaonline. it/2014/06/09/185940/osservatorio-iulm-ketchum-misurazione-della-reputazione-un-asset-strategico-per-limpresa/, date accessed 10 November 2014.

Scarpulla, F. (2008) 'Storia della Ferpi dal 1970 ad oggi' [The History of Italian Federation of PR from 1970 to This Day], unpublished Master's thesis (University of Catania, Italy).

Valentini, C. (2009) 'Italian Public Relations in a Changing World: Historical Overview, Current Questions and Future Challenges', *PRism* 6(2), http://www.prismjournal.org/fileadmin/Praxis/Files/ globalPR/VALENTINI.pdf, date accessed 27 October 2014.

Van Ruler, B. and Verčič, D. (2002) *The Bled Manifesto on Public Relations* (Ljubljana: Pristop).

DOI: 10.1057/9781137427519.0010

7
Netherlands and Belgium

Betteke van Ruler and Anne-Marie Cotton

Abstract: *Although the Flemish part of Belgium was part of the Netherlands until 1830, the countries are quite different, and that is also the case in the two parts of Belgium itself. Therefore, a brief history of public relations in the Netherlands and Belgium intersects three different stories: a story of the development of public relations as public information in the Netherlands in the 19th century; a story of public relations as propaganda and press agentry in the 20th century in the French-speaking part of Belgium; and a story of public relations as public affairs and public information in the Flemish part of the country.*

Keywords: consensus-building; Enlightenment; media relations; public affairs; public information; soft-selling persuasion

Watson, Tom (ed.). *Western European Perspectives on the Development of Public Relations: Other Voices.* Basingstoke: Palgrave Macmillan, 2015. DOI: 10.1057/9781137427519.0011.

In researching the history of PR in both countries, the perspective employed has been of the professional development and institutionalization of PR, bearing in mind Sloan's view that we are no more than just mediators of the real past (Sloan, 1991). Periodization has also been applied to deduce historical themes that have shaped the evolution of this communication discipline in neighbouring countries, which are both similar and very different for linguistic, political and social reasons.

National characteristics

With nearly 17 million and over 11 million inhabitants, respectively, the Netherlands and Belgium are among the smaller countries of Europe but are known for their major cities: Brussels, the European Union capital, and the Dutch cities of Amsterdam and The Hague.

Netherlands

Ever since the 17th century, the Netherlands has been known for its high level of wealth. People in other continents also had contact with the Dutch because of the nation's entrepreneurial nature and because of its questionable history of colonization. Over time, the Dutch built the reputation of pretending to know how people in other societies in the world should behave (Vossestein, 2001). The *Oxford Dictionary* defines a 'Dutch uncle' as one who whose manner in talking to people was 'lecturing them paternalistically' (Hofstede, 1987, p. 5). According to Vossestein, the basic values of the Dutch were always egalitarianism and a high work ethic. He claims that the Dutch have difficulty in dealing with hierarchy, always try to maintain a balance between being aware of the hierarchical aspects of a relationship and not wanting to make that awareness too obvious. Another characteristic of the Netherlands is the fragmentation of its politics. Many parties compete for electoral and parliamentary support but none of these is in a position to win a working majority on its own. This has led to a governmental system of coalitions and alliances (Kranenburg, 2001).

Belgium

Although parts of the present Belgian territory had been parts of larger entities, being among Europe's economic, political and cultural regions

DOI: 10.1057/9781137427519.0011

since the 15th century, Belgium's history goes no further than 1830. Federal Belgium is the result of a long, gradual process of territorialization of the relations between the two language groups: Flemish in the north (60 per cent of the population), and French in the south (40 per cent). As French was adopted as its single official language in 1830, this initiated the Flemish demand for 'cultural autonomy' resulting in the movement towards federalism. In the 1920s, three language areas were defined: Dutch-speaking, French-speaking and the bilingual area of Brussels. Historically a predominantly Dutch-speaking city located north of the linguistic borderline, Brussels rapidly became francophone after it was chosen as the capital city of Belgium (Baeten, 2009). According to Deschouwer (2005, p. 50), 'federalism in Belgium is thus the result not of a deliberate choice but of incremental conflict management'.

Roots of PR

PR as a profession has been evident in the Netherlands longer than in Belgium. It started in the Netherlands around 1850, in the French-speaking part of Belgium at the end of the 19th century, and in the Flemish section around 1920.

Netherlands

In the eighteenth century, science and knowledge were no longer seen as being relevant only for the elite, but had to be disseminated. This is called 'the period of Enlightenment'. The Dutch term for this diffusion was *voorlichting*, which is a literal Dutch translation of 'Enlightenment'. The idea of *voorlichting* is based on an expression of the German ethical philosopher Kant: *sapere aude* (literally, 'dare to know') and which was interpreted as 'all people must have the intention to be informed on what is going on and must be enlightened, so that they can take part in the ongoing debate about and development of society'. In the nineteenth century, the concept of *voorlichting* developed into 'giving full information to all people to mature and emancipate'. The administration as well as civil society organizations started to introduce *voorlichters*, specialists who travelled around to give information about health, good farming, housekeeping, education, politics, sexual behaviour and so on.

At the same time, the elite remained sceptical about the enlightening of ordinary people. That is why *voorlichting* was also used to show people

I

DOI: 10.1057/9781137427519.0011

how to conduct themselves as good citizens and to control them. The history of PR in the Netherlands can therefore be seen as a history of the battle between information and emancipation on the one hand, and education and persuasion on the other hand, but always under the ('Dutch uncle') dogma of 'knowing what is best'.

The characteristics of the practice of this *voorlichting* can still be seen in the daily practice of public relations departments and consultancies. The evolution of public relations in the Netherlands cannot therefore be captured in terms of 'publicity' or 'press agentry' but all the more in terms of 'public information' and well-meant (but patronizing) soft-selling 'persuasion' and 'nudging' (Lagerwey, Hemels and van Ruler, 1997). At the same time, dialogue, negotiation and consensus-building are natural exponents of Dutch culture, which for centuries has relied on the practice of consultation and the involvement of as many people as possible in decision-making (Hofstede, 1987). Every issue bearing even the remotest risk of disagreement has a forum of its own in which all interested parties are represented, whether it be traffic issues, defence matters or education affairs. Kranenburg (2001) showed that this culture has many repercussions in politics: 'The more the relevant bodies agree, the less freedom of movement remains for the politicians' (p. 38).

Belgium

Because of the new Belgian state's choice of French as its single official language in 1830, Dutch-speaking population were not a demographical but a political, sociological and psychological minority. Thus information and communication activities in Dutch cannot be found before protection against political marginalization through the new language policy was introduced – first by recognizing Dutch as the second official language and, beginning in the 1920s, delimiting the geographical areas in which Dutch or French would be the only official language. (The German-speaking community was not officially recognized until 1973. It represents 0.7 per cent of the population.) Archives, such as those of Charles de Broqueville (1870–1940), indicate that these topics emerged from the end of the 19th century onwards: public discourse, propaganda, colonial affairs, press relations, linguistic issue management and activism. According to Jacquet (1992), the propagation of PR in the different parts of Belgium resulted from economic missions of the Belgian Office for Productivity (OBAP) that was initiated by the Marshall Plan (European Recovery Program) in 1948. By collecting information on the

DOI: 10.1057/9781137427519.0011

economic and social growth of the USA during visits to companies and meetings with American CEOs and decision-makers, the participants noticed that organizations became active information and relationship agents with their environments (Ellul, 1963). They relayed in Belgium the importance for (large) organizations and (large) administrations to nurture their relations with their publics and to introduce a human dimension in their social and informational management via conferences. The first book on PR published in Belgium was *Précis de public-relations* [Handbook of public relations] written by the Swiss PR consultant Eric Cyprès (1952). It reported on the emergence of a new concept for applying publicity and information techniques, using strategies based on trust and understanding of the public's interests (Çamdereli, 2001). Its main tenets were applied by William Ugeux, director of Inforcongo (the governmental information and public relations office for Congo and Rwanda-Burundi), who aimed to positively enhance the colonial actions of Belgium in terms of health, education and infrastructures (1955–1960) in the countries (Balteau, 1997; De Vidts, 2004; Debruyne, 2008). After the independence of the Belgian Congo in 1960, Ugeux pursued the image-building of Belgium by founding Inbel, the Belgian Institute for information and documentation, in 1961 (Debruyne, 2008). He was inspired by the Dutch experience before World War II and by an institute linked to the Belgian government in exile which was based in London during World War II. Ugeux stated: 'to govern is to make information' (Gryspeerdt, 2007, p. 35). Inbel was integrated into the ministry of Foreign Affairs in 1962. It later became De Belgische Federale Voorlichtingsdienst (FVD)/Le Service Fédéral belge d'Information (SFI)/ Der Belgische Föderale Informationsdienst (FID) in 1994. Parallel to the national developments, the foundation of the European Community in Brussels transformed the new 'capital of Europe' into the cornerstone of international relations and public diplomacy (Çamdereli, 2001).

Development of the practice

As the roots of PR are different in the Netherlands and Belgium, the development of the practice was different too. In the Netherlands it was influenced by the principles of the Enlightenment and the consensus orientation of society. In Belgium PR followed different paths via appropriation or reinterpretation of the North American perspective on PR

DOI: 10.1057/9781137427519.0011

by the Catholic Social movement, which considered there was an ideological link between the Christian concept of economy and society and the American humanistic ideology of PR, and by other business trends identifying management techniques related to marketing.

Netherlands

The origins of Dutch PR practice, as noted earlier, can be found as early as in the 17th century. At that time, consular civil servants had to report regularly on the events in the country where they were stationed that might be important for shipping, trade and industry and informed government on how to cope with it. In the 18th century, civil associations hired specialized *voorlichters* to give information on, for example, better housekeeping, farming and sexual relations (Katus, 2001). After industrialization, manufacturers started to provide information on their well-being to the press as well as the general public. The first press departments, for example Jaarbeurs and the Royal Dutch Airlines KLM, originated in the beginning of the 20th century, both following the Dutch (and German) 'voorlichting' approach. The government followed soon and founded departments to inform journalists. Dutch journalists, however, preferred to keep direct access to administrators and politicians. Thanks to the strong 'pillarization' of society, with each pillar using its own media and therefore its own political contacts, their lobby was successful for a long time and the governmental PR departments were forced to aim their press releases to foreign journalists only.

Moreover, according to Kickert (1996), the Netherlands was seen as an almost perfect example of the modern non-state concept of what he calls 'neo-corporatism'. This European model emphasized the interests of a small, fixed number of well-organized interest groups that were recognized by the state which gave them privilege or even monopoly. Usually, the most important groups in a corporatist society are employers, employees and the state. However, in the Netherlands, all kinds of single-issue pressure groups were also involved in the system.

These characteristics have influenced PR practice. Civil society is seen as the basis of society-building in the Netherlands and pressure groups are a natural part of life. This was due to the consensus-building nature of the Dutch and pillarization and corporatism, therefore, never led to a strongly polarized society, even in the turbulent 1960s (see Kickert, 1996 for an overview). Moreover, pressure groups have been allowed great

DOI: 10.1057/9781137427519.0011

involvement in decision-making, in politics and nowadays also in the corporate arena, as long as they are not too violent in their approach. That is why cooperation is an important strategy of Dutch pressure groups. Van Luijk, Professor in Business Ethics in the Netherlands, calls it 'democratisation of moral authority' (van Luijk and Schilder, 1997, p. 3), and it has become normal part of life. As a result, aggressive persuasion is not an acceptable PR strategy. Although management styles are changing and 'Americanizing', so that competition is more common, dialogue is often used for soft-selling and patronizing reasons.

The Dutch have one of the oldest PR professional associations founded in 1947 (then called NGPR, Het Nederlands Genootschap Public Relations en Voorlichting [Dutch Association of Public Relations and Enlightenment, now called Logeion). It was soon followed by more specialized associations for governmental and hospital PR, public affairs and regional networks (Lagerwey, Hemels and van Ruler, 1997).

Belgium

The roots of PR can be found in propaganda which was linked to the industries derived from the Belgian colonial activities, involving companies as well as the government (Stanard, 2012), public affairs (linguistic and political issues from the beginning of the 20th century) and media relations (relaying information). PR practitioners wanted to be considered by journalists as the preferred gatekeepers for relevant information (Van Bol and Ugeux, 1983). Therefore departments dedicated to the systematic dissemination of information were created in both public institutions and companies before these practices were introduced more widely from the US after World War II.

The first proper PR departments were, however, only established after the war at companies, such as the Belgian branch of Esso (1946), the insurance firm Caisse Nationale Belge d'Assurance/Algemene Verzekeringen (1949) and the Société Générale de Belgique/Generale Bankmaatschappij, a bank (1950) (Pauwels and van Gorp, 2004).

The creation of the Belgian Center for Public Relations/Belgisch Center voor Public Relations (BCPR)/Centre Belge de Relations Publiques (CBRP) in 1953 by Victor Snutsel (Shell President), Eric Cyprès (PR consultant), Jean de Broux (General Insurance), Pierre Janssen (Esso), Robert Maillard (Sabena), Jacques Overloop (IBM), Joe Cavillot (GM), Fernand Huybrechts (Ford) and Robert Goeman (Philips) played an

DOI: 10.1057/9781137427519.0011

important role in the professionalization and institutionalization of PR in Belgium by bringing together in-house practitioners from private or public institutions with consultants (Çamdereli, 2001). It organized IPRA's first world congress on 25–27 June 1958 in Brussels with the motto of 'Public Relations in the Service of Mankind' with 237 delegates from 23 countries (Centre Belge des Relations Publiques, 1958). Together with French, Italian and Dutch associations, BCPR established the European Confederation of Public Relations (CERP) in 1959 in Orléans (France) but headquartered in Brussels (Çamdereli, 2001). The BCPR changed into 3C Corporate Communication Community, in 2007, endorsing the evolution of PR from relations with publics to organizational communication and 'supporting business development in different ways: from internal change management to attracting new employees, to reputation management' (3C, 2014).

The Belgian Public Relations Consultants Association (BPRCA), formed in 1990, represents 28 top Belgian consultancies, ranging from independent agencies to international network consultancies, and monitors its members' observance of a code of ethics. It conforms to the Stockholm Charter, which was adopted in 2003 and replaced the Rome Charter adopted by International Communication Consultants Organisation (ICCO) in 1986. Its members provide strategic advice to local and multinational organizations and institutions (BPRCA, 2014).

At national level, there are more associations: the Belgian Investor Relations Association (BIRA), the Belgian associations for internal communication (BViC and ABCi) and the association for public information (Kortom) since 2000. This fragmentation, on one hand, reflects the ongoing professionalization of the field and, on the other, the complex identity problem that PR suffers from.

Development of education and research

Education and research are flourishing in both countries, with many research and applied university courses and curricula.

Netherlands

The first courses in PR were offered as optional courses at a university level as early as in the late 1940s, always under the umbrella of 'mass communication' and 'journalism'. PR was presented as 'working for the

DOI: 10.1057/9781137427519.0011

public, with the public, and in public', and thus perceived as a function of the larger societal communication system (van Ruler and Verčič, 2005). In this societal approach, PR serves the same kind of (democratic) function as journalism does, as both contribute to the free flow of information and its interpretations, and the development of the public sphere. For a long time education and research stayed closely related to that in journalism; not because the practitioners have to deal with journalists, but because of these overlapping functions in society (van der Meiden, 1978). This has changed (van Ruler, 1996). Both education and research are nowadays approached from a management perspective and, as a result, research changed direction to investigate effects of certain PR approaches to publics but not the unintended sociological (unintended) consequences of PR activities in society. PR research can be found at 13 research universities but in very different departments such as economics, business, mass communication, speech, agriculture, design, but never under the heading 'public relations'. This is also the case in education: curricula are called 'communication' or 'corporate communication'.

Belgium

Because of its political scenario, Belgium offers a complex situation in its education systems. Historically, they reflected the linguistic battles and there is a strong differentiation between academic and professional programmes.

PR has been taught as a professional bachelor degree since 1970 at six institutes of higher education in Flanders (one per province) and at eight institutes of higher education in the French community. The French programmes adopt an operational approach with an emphasis on tactics, writing and presentation skills, and the dimension of citizenship, while the Dutch programmes additionally integrate the managerial dimension into their curriculum (van Ruler and Verčič 2004) and combine PR and *voorlichting*.

However, the first communication courses dedicated to the history of the press, press laws, ethics and techniques were offered at academic/ university level in 1946 at the political and social sciences school of the Catholic University of Leuven/Louvain (UCL) and in 1948 at the Brussels University (ULB) (Lits, 1999). They resulted from discussions held in London during World War II by William Ugeux, Marc Delforge and Paul Lévy who developed a draft of a 'Institut des Techniques de Diffusion'. From 1945 onwards, the rector of UCL sought to introduce these courses

DOI: 10.1057/9781137427519.0011

(Balteau, 1997). Emerging from these 'techniques of diffusion' and media studies, a dedicated course in dissemination techniques and PR was created during 1957–1958 at the UCL School of Political Science, together with the PR department of the university (which became Press and *Voorlichting* in 1966, and communication in 1995). After 1968 and the linguistic crisis in the country, the French scholars left Leuven and migrated to a brand new city, Louvain-la-Neuve in 1975; however, both Flemish (KUL) and French (UCL) kept PR in their curriculum (Gryspeerdt, 2007). In 1990, UCL, together with the Université de Liège, created a research group bringing all French-speaking PR researchers together. UCL also initiated a research laboratory, Laboratoire d'Analyse des Systèmes de Communication des Organisations (LASCO), thus extending the PR education and research questions to the entire French-speaking community, including France and Québec. The education landscape is facing new challenges as comprehensive reform has taken place with the *Décret Marcourt*, creating a single Académie d'Enseignement Supérieur et de Recherche (ARES) bringing universities and *hautes écoles* together. PR is presently taught through a set of different theoretical approaches at the French-speaking universities with a strong accent on organizational communication.

In Flanders, PR is mentioned less in the academic curricula of its four universities, as the Dutch traditions are followed with emphasis on *voorlichting*, corporate communication and strategic communication, information and persuasion beside journalism and media studies. The link between the Netherlands and Flanders, forged by academic publications and books by Guido Fauconnier (Leuven) and Anne van der Meiden (Utrecht), has been institutionalized through the NVAO (Nederlands-Vlaamse Accreditatieorganisatie) [Netherlands–Flanders Accreditation Organisation] which has brought more uniformity in the education.

At the European level, Belgium played an important role as CERP Education was initiated by Jos Willems (director of Hoger Instituut voor Bedrijfsopleidingen, HIBO, Ghent, the first institute of higher education offering a bachelor in public relations in Flanders) at the end of the 1980s. CERP Education organized the first European seminar for PR teachers, researchers and practitioners. It was titled as 'Public Relations in the Future: From Theory to Practice' and held in Bruges in 1990 (Willems, 1990). CERP became EUPRERA (European Public Relations Education and Research Association) in 2000. Willems also launched a Master's in European Public Relations (MARPE) with university partners in several European countries, which continues (2014).

DOI: 10.1057/9781137427519.0011

Current issues

Netherlands

Looking at the historical development and using a professional perspective (Sloan, 1991), we may conclude that the field of 'communication', as it is called in the Netherlands, is widely accepted and acts at a strategic level in most organizations. Almost all organizations have 'communication employees' or at least structural contacts with communication consultancies. Managers see communication as an important, or even as a critical, factor for success. An official commission advised the Prime Minister on how to cope with communication in the new information age and follow-up commissions are very well institutionalized.

Nowadays, the sector strives for more planning of communication activities and introduced SCRUM as a planning method (van Ruler, 2014). Governmental communication professionals have introduced a 'Silver Standard' several years ago, which stipulates that all campaigns must be evaluated; there is growing attention in the profession for evaluation methods, especially for follow-up decision-making in campaigning. The debate in the professional journals and at congresses, however, concentrates on strategic counselling and mentoring/coaching roles. These are seen as the new challenges of the profession. This goes hand in hand with a discussion on the identity of the profession and the need to research the profession from a more sociological, historical perspective.

Belgium

As in the Netherlands and the rest of Europe, Belgium faces fundamental changes in the different spheres of human activities. To guarantee their development, organizations have to adapt to the knowledge revolution as well as to the public's evolution towards the self-expression of their opinions in a public space becoming more virtual and interactive (Maisonneuve, 2010). The globalization also enhances the adoption of similar communication systems, including tools as monitoring, score cards and so on. Belgian PR agencies definitively position themselves as strategic partners with similar aims as their Dutch homologues in terms of strategic advice and coaching. The challenges focus on evaluation and return on investment, and on transparency and ethics for the lobby industry in Brussels.

DOI: 10.1057/9781137427519.0011

Historical development

Although historical developments are often difficult to relate to precise periods, a timeline of developments in the Netherlands and Belgium can be indicated, as follows.

Pre-period

In the 18th and 19th centuries, the first traces of PR can be found in the Netherlands in two different forms: first, by the *voorlichters* who were employed by Dutch non-profit organizations to provide information on farming, health, housekeeping, budgeting, sexuality and so on. Second, by civil servants who were employed to inform government about developments in the moods and opinions of leaders in industry and trade sectors. Nevertheless, we cannot call this two-way PR, as these two streets were located at totally different levels and/or organizations. Although *voorlichting* can be seen as the basis of PR in later years, this was a 'pre-period', mainly focused on attempting to bring Enlightenment.

The Belgian situation was slightly different as its history only starts in 1830 with the separation from the Netherlands. Until World War I, French as the dominant language determined the publics involved in the dominant coalition: politicians, bankers and captains of industry. By the end of the 19th century, union movements, Flemish nationalist movements and the press (becoming the voice of the different political streams) joined the debates.

First period

In the 1920s the first Dutch press departments were established within industry and government, oriented at enlightening journalists by informing them about what was going on in the respective organizations. Here the beginning of understanding of the benefits and necessity of public information is demonstrated. Yet, although ideology called for full information and 'telling the truth', practice showed that this was a bridge too far and was restricted to 'telling the ideal story'.

Press relations commenced in a similar way in Belgium. Beside information dissemination about organizations as an increasingly common practice, PR-like activity by linguistic lobby resulted in the recognition of Dutch as the second national language (1898) – the principle of territoriality for both language communities (1921) and the language legislation (1932).

DOI: 10.1057/9781137427519.0011

Second period

In 1946, the first association of professionals NGPR, Nederlands Genootschap voor Public Relations (Dutch Association of Public Relations; now called Logeion), was established. Soon it was followed by a still-existing network of directors in advertising and PR: Kring 48 (Society 48). This constituted the commencement of institutionalization of the profession, which from then on was mainly called public relations and *voorlichting*, or public relations and *reclame* (advertising).

Belgium followed with the creation of the BCPR, Belgian Center for Public Relations, in 1953. As several international organizations chose Brussels as their headquarters (e.g. NATO, European Union), it also became a central location for the further development of European PR associations. Belgium is one of the first European countries to add communication into the academic curriculum with the launch of the first communication courses in 1946 at the political and social sciences school of the Catholic University of Leuven/Louvain and in 1948 at the Brussels University.

Third period

The third period in the Netherlands was a period of professionalization. The year 1964 marked the first academic chair in Voorlichtingskunde (often translated as education science, but is more accurately expressed as Enlightenment science). In 1976, Dr Anne van der Meiden became the first Professor in PR, appointed to a special NGPR-sponsored chair at the University of Utrecht. Soon after (1978) the first BA programme started at the Hogeschool Eindhoven applied university (now Fontys) to be followed by many courses elsewhere and at different levels. Based on a government report (Openbaarheid Openheid, 1970), in 1980, the first Law on Public Information was established, stating that the government was obliged to be open and transparent in every detail unless security and privacy prohibited it.

According to Gritti (1999), World War II propaganda initiated concepts such as 'mass' and 'crowd'; opinion leaders and influencers were introduced to communication strategies using audio-visual supports to persuade publics. Lohisse (1999) describes the 1970s in Belgium as a key transition period for communication studies as two major shifts occurred: (1) the shift of paradigm from 'ideal status' to 'real acts'; and (2) a shift to language analysis as a social activity, studying the integration of situational factors and communication processes: contextualized communication

DOI: 10.1057/9781137427519.0011

became a research topic, and empirical research addressed individuals and organizations in their networked and contextual complexity.

Fourth period

From the 1980s onwards, the profession showed rapid growth. The name of the profession changed from 'public relations' and *voorlichting* to 'corporate communication' or simply 'communication'. By 2000 most Dutch organizations with over 50 employees had at least one or two 'communication professionals'. There were three reasons: (1) the introduction of the corporate communication concept by Cees van Riel, a Dutch PR scholar; (2) the poor image of the PR profession caused by its non-transparency, specially scrutinized by journalists; (3) changing ideas about the concept of *voorlichting*.

Communication became a societal challenge where the dominant merchandising of 'communication goods' and supremacy of private companies' interests over governments' were increasingly present. Utopian critiques of the 1960s were gradually replaced by a 'professionalist communication ideology' which was also implemented in academic programmes (Proulx, 1999).

Fifth period

Also around 2000, governmental and business campaigning suffered from an identity crisis due to the arrival of digitalization and changed societal attitudes. In this period, image-building came under pressure because of the (unforeseen) combination with a general decline of trust. The answer to this was the invention of, and switch-over, to new rules: responsiveness, transparency, identity and dialogue, and next to this the role of PR in journalistic concepts such as branded journalism and the like.

Here was a change in theory and practice: from instrumental orchestration of utterances in order to change knowledge, moods and behaviours of target groups into the concept of the reflective and adaptive practitioner who is there to coach others to communicate well.

References

3C – Corporate Communications Community (2014) 'Mission Statement', http://www.3c.be/fr/about-us/mission-3c/, data accessed 30 October 2014.

DOI: 10.1057/9781137427519.0011

Baeten, G. (2009) 'Territorialising Brussels: Belgian Devolution and the Spatial Conundrum of a Bilingual Capital', in J. Anderson (ed.) *Divided Cities/Contested States*, Working Paper 14, 4–20, http://www. conflictincities.org/PDFs/WorkingPaper14_29.1.10.pdf, date accessed 30 October 2014.

Balteau, B. (1997) *William Ugeux. Un témoin du siècle* [William Ugeux: A Century's Witness] (Bruxelles: Racine).

Bol, J-M., van, and Ugeux, W. (1983) *Les relations publiques: responsabilité du management* [Public Relations: Management's Responsibility] (Paris: F. Nathan).

BPRCA – Belgian Public Relations Consultants Association (2014) 'Mission and Values', http://www.bprca.be/site/index. php?option=com_content&view=article&id=8&lang=en, date accessed 30 October 2014.

Çamdereli, M. (2001) 'Dünden Bugüne Belçika'da Halkla İlişkiler' [Public Relations from Yesterday to Today in Belgium], *Istanbul University Faculty of Communications Magazine*, 10, 281–310.

Centre Belge des Relations Publiques (1958) *Les relations publiques au service de l'homme: actes du premier congrès mondial des relations publiques: Bruxelles, 25-26-27 juin 1958* [Public Relations in the Service of Mankind: Proceedings of the First Public Relations World Congress: Brussels, 25–27 June 1958] (Brussels: BPRC).

Cyprès, E. (1952) *Précis de public-relations* [Public Relations Guide Book] (Bruxelles: Librairie des Sciences).

Debruyne, E. (2008) *La guerre secrète des espions belges: 1940–1944* [The Secret War of Belgian Spies: 1940–1944] (Bruxelles: Racine).

Deschouwer, K. (2005) 'Kingdom of Belgium', in J. Kincaid and G. Alan Tarr (eds) *Constitutional Origins, Structure, and Change in Federal Countries*, Volume 1 of Global Dialogue on Federalism (Montreal & Kingston: McGill-Queen's University Press, 2005), 49–75.

De Vidts, K. (2004) 'Belgium a Small yet Significant Resistance Force during World War II', unpublished Master's dissertation (Hawaii Pacific University, Honolulu, USA).

Ellul, J. (1963) De la signification des relations publiques dans la société technicienne [Meaning of Public Relations in a Technician Society] *l'Année sociologique 1963* [Sociological Annual 1963] (Paris: Presse Universitaire de France).

Gritti, J. (1999) 'Les années cinquante dans les recherches en communication' [The Fifties and Communication Research],

DOI: 10.1057/9781137427519.0011

in M. Lits (ed.) *Un demi-siècle d'études en communication* [Half a Century in Communication Studies], Volume 11 of Recherches en Communication, (Louvain-la-Neuve, April 1999), 21–42.

Gryspeerdt, A. (2007) 'Catholicisme et communication en Belgique' [Catholicism and Communication in Belgium], *Hermès, La Revue*, 48, 33–38.

Hofstede, G. (1987) 'Gevolgen van het Nederlanderschap: gezondheid, recht en economie' [The Results of Dutch Citizenship: Health, Justice and Economy], Inaugural lecture (University of Maastricht, Netherlands).

Jacquet, S. (1992) 'Catholicisme social et relations publiques. Éléments pour une histoire des relations publiques en Belgique dans les années 50 et 60' [Social Catholicism and Public Relations. Parts of a Public Relations' History in Belgium in the Fifties and the Sixties], unpublished Master's dissertation (Université de Liège, Belgium).

Katus, J. (2001) 'Government Communication: Development, Functions and Principles' in J. Katus and F. Volmer (eds) *Government Communication in the Netherlands* (The Hague: SDU).

Kickert, W J. M. (1996) 'Expansion and Diversification of Public Administration in the Postwar Welfare State: The Case of the Netherlands', *Public Administration Review*, 1.

Kranenburg, M. (2001) 'The Political Wing of the "Polder Model", in M. Kranenburg (ed.) *The Netherlands: A Practical Guide for the Foreigner and a Mirror for the Dutch* (Amsterdam and Rotterdam: Prometheus and NRC Handelsblad).

Lagerwey, E., Hemels, J. and van Ruler, B. (1997) *Op Zoek Naar Faamwaarde: Vijftig Jaar Public Relations in Nederland* [Searching Fame's Value: Fifty Years of Public Relations in the Netherlands] (Houten: Bohn Stafleu Van Loghum).

Lits, M. (1999) 'Cinquante années de recherches en communication' [Fifty Years of Communication Research], in M. Lits (ed.) *Un demi-siècle d'études en communication* [Half a Century in Communication Studies], Volume 11 of Recherches en Communication (Louvain-la-Neuve, April 1999), 9–19.

Lohisse, J. (1999) 'La construction de la communication' [Building Communication], in M. Lits (ed.) *Un demi-siècle d'études en communication* [Half a Century in Communication Studies], Volume 11 of Recherches en Communication (Louvain-la-Neuve, April 1999), 59–66.

DOI: 10.1057/9781137427519.0011

Luijk, H. van and Schilder, A. (1997) *Patronen van verantwoordelijkheid: ethiek en corporate governance* [Patterns of Responsibility: Ethics and Corporate Governance] (Schoonhoven: Academic Service).

Maisonneuve, D. (2010) *Les relations publiques dans une société en mouvance* [Public Relations in a Transformation Society] (Sainte-Foy, PUQ).

Meiden, A. van der (1978) 'Wat zullen de mensen ervan zeggen? Enkele visies op het publiek in de ontwikkelingsgang van de public relations' [What Will People Say? Some Views of the Public in the Development of Public Relations], Inaugural lecture, University of Utrecht (The Hague: NGPR).

Openbaarheid Openheid (1970) *Rapport van de Commissie heroriëntatie overheidsvoorlichting* [Report of the Commission on Reorientation on Governmental Englightenment] ('s Gravenhage: Staatsuitgeverij).

Pauwels, L. and Gorp, B. van (2004) 'Belgium', in B. van Ruler and D. Verčič (eds) *Public Relations and Communication Management in Europe: A Nation-by-Nation Introduction to Public Relations Theory and Practice* (Berlin: Walter de Gruyter).

Proulx (1999), 'La pensée communicationnelle dans les années soixante-dix: critique des médias et émergence de nouvelles alternatives' [The Communication Tough in the Seventies: Media Critics and Emergence of New Alternatives], in M. Lits (ed.) *Un demi-siècle d'études en communication* [Half a Century in Communication Studies], Volume 11 of Recherches en Communication (Louvain-la-Neuve, April 1999), 67–79.

Ruler, B. van (1996) 'Communicatiemanagement in Nederland' [Communication Management in the Netherlands]. Dissertation (Houten: Bohn Stafleu Van Loghum).

Ruler, B. van (2014) *Reflective Communication Scrum* (The Hague: Eleven).

Ruler, B. van and Verčič, D. (eds) (2004) *Public Relations and Communication Management in Europe: A Nation-by-Nation Introduction to Public Relations Theory and Practice* (Berlin: Walter de Gruyter).

Sloan, W. D. (1991) *Perspectives on Mass Communication History* (Mahwah, NJ: Lawrence Erlbaum).

Stanard, M. (2012) *Selling the Congo: A History of European Pro-empire Propaganda and the Making of Belgian Imperialism* (Lincoln: University of Nebraska Press).

DOI: 10.1057/9781137427519.0011

Vossestein, J. (2001) *Dealing with the Dutch: The Cultural Context of Business and Work in the Netherlands in the Early 21st Century* (Amsterdam: KIT Publishers).

Willems, J. (ed.) (1990) 'Public Relations in the Future: From Theory to Practice', Proceedings of the first European Seminar to teach teachers, researchers and practitioners, 1–3 November (Gent: HIBO).

DOI: 10.1057/9781137427519.0011

8
Scandinavia

Abstract: *Scandinavia is a region in Northern Europe consisting of three relatively homogeneous countries, namely Sweden, Norway and Denmark. For centuries, these countries and their populations have formed a social, economic, political, and last, but not least, a linguistic community. Despite this homogeneity, the discipline of public relations (PR) has not developed along the same track in Scandinavia. In Sweden, for example, PR started within state authorities and the first association for Swedish press officers working in the public sector was established in 1950. In Norway, the Norwegian Public Relations Club was created almost at the same time, in 1949. However, the Norwegian Labour Party was inspired by American PR ideas earlier, in the 1930s. In Denmark, the Danish Public Relations Club was not established until 1961, and its first members were all recruited from private companies.*

Keywords: Denmark; Norway; Scandinavia; Sweden

Watson, Tom (ed.). *Western European Perspectives on the Development of Public Relations: Other Voices*. Basingstoke: Palgrave Macmillan, 2015. DOI: 10.1057/9781137427519.0012.

Sweden

Larsåke Larsson

Public relations (PR) started in Sweden during World War II and developed significantly a couple of decades thereafter, even though a few organizations (military headquarters, the central trade union and the federation of farmers) ran such activities to a lesser extent before the war, mostly in the form of press relations. The subsequent development can be linked with industry's need for better relations with society, the rise of interest organizations and the expansion of public administration and service at national, regional and local level (Larsson, 2005).

When war began in 1939, the Swedish government established an information office (National Information Bureau) at department level. To begin with, two former journalists were appointed as the first Swedish PR officers. The information bureau was given the task of informing the general public about war matters and to oversee what was published about the war in the media. Soon a task to 'strengthen the resistance power of the civil population' was also added. The mission thus was twofold: first, to inform society and, second, to control and manage the press. In principle, the media was not to print improper facts. The bureau wrote and disseminated thousands of articles about different war matters to the press for this purpose. The information mission involved, due to the bureau's instructions, the production of different forms of propaganda (SNA, 2005).

Sweden was a non-belligerent in World War II, though it came very close to being occupied by Nazi German (as happened to neighbouring Denmark and Norway). At the same time it became isolated concerning trade and import of vital materials. The information bureau's task included warnings to be vigilant for spies and calls to be secret about any military-type occurrences under the motto 'A Swede keeps silent'. As the country was isolated and lacked import of raw goods, propaganda included a variety of campaigns about housekeeping and material supplying for the industry (as how to produce coffee and tyres, use the forest's food resources and collect metal goods and scrap metal) (SNA, 2005).

By the end of, and just after, the war a small number of organizations had established public relations functions and hired PR personnel, for

DOI: 10.1057/9781137427519.0012

example, Swedish Post, Swedish Rail, the Cooperative Society together with some private companies, among them the new air carrier Scandinavian Airlines System (SAS).

In 1950, the PR occupational population consisted of 30 people, most working in state and government agencies and enterprises, such as the rail and post authorities and the National Board of Health. Almost all called themselves press officers. All were men. Contacts with the press were their primary task. Thus, a distinctive feature of the Swedish PR history compared with many other countries is that PR started within state authorities and was in line with the development and growth of the governmental sector at different levels. In this same year, 1950, the first organization was established for this group, Swedish Press Officers Association. Ten years later the name was changed to Swedish Public Relations Association, by then with around 100 members (Larsson, 2005).

The first consulting PR firms in Sweden, a couple of one-man bureaux, came into being in the late 1950s. They combined PR and advertising. A few new firms were established over the next decade, but their number remained low well into the 1970s.

In the 1960s, the PR industry developed rather slowly. However, several private companies together with their business association hired PR specialists to deal with different communication problems that trade and industry experienced. One was the socialization and anti-capitalist debate at this time; another was the start of a very active environmental movement in society opposing, for example, chemical spraying in the forestry industry and contamination by the paper mills. At the end of the decade, Sweden faced the same radical left political opposition, as many other countries in the continent, with demonstrations and occupations.

In the 1970s, PR developed faster than in the previous decade. The body of PR officers grew as information units and departments were established in many organizations, above all in the public sector. In line with the expansion of the public sector (childcare, education, medical care etc.) public authorities and agencies at national and especially regional and local levels now hired many employees with PR competence. Around 400 PR officers worked in these agencies in the middle of the decade, twice as many as ten years earlier (Larsson, 2005).

In the public and private/business sector, the PR professional group totalled around 1500 persons in this period. Some 600 of them were members of the Swedish Public Relations Association. In 1975, a parallel organization was founded for those working in the public sector as they felt that SPRA was too focused on private-sector matters.

Communication operations in both private and public organizations were normally performed in-house by their own staff, while PR bureaus still were a rather rare phenomenon; in the middle of the 1970s, only some ten firms were to be found with around 25 consultants.

The 1980s can be seen as a transition period in several aspects. The number of PR/information workers increased, but only to a limited extent. Working methods and professionalism developed, not least based on many new PR officers receiving higher education and training on the recently introduced university PR/information courses. A third aspect was the transition from in-house operations to the engagement of external consultants for many operations.

Not until the end of the 1980s did a 'real' consulting trade with companies offering a broader service base begin to take shape. Most companies were established by people coming from the political sphere, primarily conservative parties and think tanks as well as business organizations. Some large international PR firms also established offices, or bought into companies in Sweden (e.g. Burson-Marsteller and Hill & Knowlton). The Swedish Public Relations Association (SPRA) and the PR association for the public sector merged in 1992 while the name for the united organization was changed to The Swedish Information Association. (The acronym SPRA was, however, maintained internationally.)

In the 1990s, conditions for organizational communication work changed significantly. Sweden experienced a long economic boom and the country was transformed to a more market-oriented society. Contacts and cooperation with Europe were intensified for many corporations and organizations. The information technology industry grew rapidly. The working forms and conditions for PR officers changed with the arrival of e-mail and Internet. As in most other countries there were suddenly a number of new communication channels to use.

The market for PR consulting services expanded and several PR bureaus were established, often relatively small at first but growing very rapidly. Mergers, acquisitions and breakups were common at this time (and still are). The industry was visibly volatile. In this climate, the larger Swedish PR companies grew quite steadily. The PR/information industry as a whole expanded heavily and the body of PR professionals increased, especially in the private sector. In the middle of the decade a total of 6000–7000 people were engaged in organizational communication work. 'It was like an explosion, we recruited all people to be found', one PR company leader recalled in an interview about the development of the PR trade (Larsson, 2005).

The development and growth of the Swedish PR industry was thus above all a result of a marked shift in the political system beginning in the later 1980s. Once a country with an evident corporative political system, where different interest groups were represented in government bodies, Sweden changed to a more liberal market-oriented society. Whereas these groups (businesses, unions and other organizations) previously participated as members in state committees and expressed their opinions in a solid remittance system, they now had to seek influence through lobbying, mass media, opinion building and other means (Larsson, 2006).

Higher education in PR also developed significantly in the 1990s. All universities together with many colleges expanded their one-year course (started in the 1970s) to full three-year bachelor-level programmes, named Media and Communication Studies.

The new millennium started with a decline for the PR industry. A year into the new millennium Sweden experienced a deep recession, especially for the information technology industry, resulting in a reduced need for communication specialists and PR consultants. Three to four years passed before the PR industry was back to where it was at the start of the millennium. During the previous decade, the PR world increased although development has taken a slower pace than in the 1990s.

Today (2015), the PR industry in Sweden is estimated to comprise 12,000–15,000 practitioners. The share of consultants is comparatively low; one out of seven works in a consultancy firm, while the rest are employed as staff in companies, public authorities and organizations. Three of four of the total professional group are women and almost one in two PR managers is a woman. A special feature of the Swedish PR landscape has been the relatively large share of practitioners in the public sector, owing to the size of this sector in the country (Flodin, 2004; Larsson, 2005). Almost half of the total number of PR practitioners is estimated to work in public-sector units. Of the total membership of 6100 members in the professional association, now with the new name Swedish Association of Communication Professionals, 33 per cent work in the private sector (companies) while 40 per cent are employed in the public sector (government and state/local/regional authorities and companies), leaving 27 per cent working in interest organizations and consulting firms (Johansson and Larsson, forthcoming).

DOI: 10.1057/9781137427519.0012

References

Flodin, B. (2004) 'Sweden', in B. van Ruler and D. Verčič (eds) *Public Relations and Communication Management in Europe* (Berlin: Mouton de Gruyter).

Johansson, B. and Larsson, L. (forthcoming) 'The Complexity of Public Relations Work: PR Manager's Composite Role: The Swedish Case', *Nordicom Review*.

Larsson, L. (2005) *Upplysning och propaganda. Utvecklingen av svensk PR och information* [Information and Propaganda: The Development of Swedish PR] (Lund: Studentlitteratur)

Larsson, L. (2006) 'Public Relations and Democracy: The Swedish Case', in J. L'Etang and M. Pieczka (eds) *Public Relations: Critical Debates and Contemporary Practice* (Mahwah, NJ: Lawrence Erlbaum)

SNA – The Swedish National Archives (2005) *The State Information Bureau: Documents 1939–1945*.

DOI: 10.1057/9781137427519.0012

Norway

Tor Bang

The Norsk [Norwegian] Public Relations Club was founded in 1949 by a group of 'powerful and elite Norwegian public sector leaders' (Warner-Søderholm and Bang, 2013, p. 39). However, the history of the modern notion of PR practice can be traced back to the early 1930s, when Arbeiderpartiet, the Labour Party, developed, implemented and launched election campaigns based on principles of modern PR with carefully defined stakeholder groups. The field's post-war history is well documented by Warner-Søderholm and Bang (2013), Ihlen and Robstad (2004) and Bang and Rød (2003). Ihlen (2013) discusses boundaries of 'public relations', where he argues that the broader term 'strategic communication' involves 'public relations', as well as organizational communication and marketing communication. Discussing PR in pre-20th-century contexts requires contemporary connotations of 'PR'.

Leaning on Ihlen (2013) and Bernays (1923, 1928, 1952), this section reviews pre-20th-century PR practices in Norway framed within the realm of 'public relations' in two sections and an afterword: (1) Anecdotal knowledge in rural Norway of 'potetprester', public-information campaigns on potato growing from the 1760s; (2) The work of Henrik Wergeland, an early 19th-century lobbyist who challenged the 1814 Constitution §2 which forbade Jews from entering the country; (3) Nobel laureate Bjørnstjerne Bjørnson, best known for putting his rhetorical and oratory skills in promoting small nations' emancipation in 19th-century Europe who was Henrik Wergeland's 'spin doctor'.

Potetprester: 18th-century public-information campaigns

Ministers of the Danish–Norwegian Lutheran church are sometimes referred to as 'potato priests' (potetprester), essentially a derogatory term, though not without connotations of pastoral fathers lovingly caring for their rural congregations. The term was coined by parishioners of Peder Harboe Hertzberg (1728–1802). With the advent of the Age of Enlightenment, social radicalism entered the public sphere. Poverty

DOI: 10.1057/9781137427519.0012

could be seen as a structural problem, not necessarily God's will. Witnessing parishioners victimized by famine, Hertzberg developed a public-information campaign to encourage peasants to grow potatoes and thus fight starvation. Hertzberg, followed by hundreds of fellow clergymen, thus responded to religious imperatives, as well as decrees given by the Danish crown, which ruled Norway.

Potatoes had for some time been grown in aristrocrats' gardens as ornamental plants. However, there was little knowledge among common people as to what parts that were edible, and potatoes were therefore shown little interest.

A self-taught botanist, Hertzberg started to grow potatoes in 1758 in the vicarage garden in Bømlo, on the Atlantic coast of south-western Norway. He shared his insight with parishioners, lecturing on the blessings of potatoes from his pulpit, as well as seeking families and hamlets in need of improving their nutrition in 'uår' ['un-years' – years of famine]. Potatoes are easy to grow, even in harsh climates. They are full of nutrition, filling and hinder scurvy, a deficiency disease stemming from malnutrition and lack of vitamin C. In 1763, Hertzberg published a handbook about growing and using potatoes, a step-by-step guide, written in simple Danish–Norwegian for a broad readership. The handbook proved to be popular. In its second edition (1773) he included stories on economic success of farmers who had marketed and sold their surplus: 15,000 barrels of potatoes to the German regiment in Bergen.

This knowledge, diffused among poorly educated parishioners, may have been instrumental in saving tens of thousands of Norwegians from death by starvation during the Napoleonic wars when British ships imposed an embargo on Norwegian ports, cutting off vital imports from Denmark. When grain crops failed due to an exceptionally short growing season in 1808, there was widespread famine in areas where farmers had not learned to grow the crop.

The potetprest campaigns could have been designed according to the 21st-century text books: they defined short- and long-term goals of hindering starvation, and improving social conditions, as well as several objectives en route, such as teaching peasants how to grow potatoes and reducing infant mortality. Another goal was to industrialize farming, thus enabling peasants to partake in a semi-capitalist urban economy, a skill already developed in coastal areas by small-scale 'fiskebønder' [fishermen-peasants]. Campaigns were designed strategically and tactically, using communication channels available at the time, including lectures,

DOI: 10.1057/9781137427519.0012

handbooks and the unchallenged parish vicars' ethos, preaching from pulpits, which was probably the most effective campaign tool. Evaluating the outcome, they were highly successful, although not measurable quantitatively.

Henrik Wergeland: 19th-century human rights activist and lobbyist

Towards the end of the Napoleonic war and amid the reconstruction of the European political map, Norway was given as war reparation from the Danish crown to Sweden. It was able to negotiate domestic autonomy with Sweden, resulting in an 1814 Constitution. The Constitution §2 was popularly named 'Jødeparagrafen' for the 'paragraph to ban Jews' from entering the country.

The goal of Henrik Wergeland (1808–1845), Norway's best-known poet was to revoke §2. With the help of parliamentarian Hans Holmboe, the rector of *Bergen Katedralskole*, Wergeland unsuccessfully petitioned Stortinget, the national assembly, for a change in 1839. In two pamphlets about 'Jødesagen', the Jewish issue, 'Indlæg i Jødesagen' (1841) and 'Jødesagen i det norske Storthing' (1842), he lobbied politicians about the inconsistency that governed the law. No other nationalities were imposed with travel and entry restrictions and he lamented that 'Turks and heathens are free to travel in our land, but Jews, once God's chosen people,... honored as mother for the sacred religion to which we confess, should like a defiled and unholy nation be kept from us' (1842). He argued that Jews were indeed not only *The Chosen*, but they were selected and defined as outcast by Norwegian constitutionalists. There had been exceptions: Stortinget had elected to turn a blind eye to §2 when in 1822 the young nation, on the verge of bankruptcy, needed to refinance its national debts. Joseph Hambro from Copenhagen, and Vilhelm Benedicks from Stockholm, both Jewish, were invited to Norway to negotiate new credits. 'Portugiserjøder', Sephardic Jews, were from time to time granted visas if their services were needed, a continuation of the 1687 law on Jews entering the Kingdom.

Wergeland was moderately successful in his lifetime. In response to his petition, Stortinget agreed to a vote in 1842, resulting in a simple majority for revoking the ban. Wergeland saw that as a major victory. While battling with tuberculosis, he wrote two of the best-known poems

DOI: 10.1057/9781137427519.0012

in the Norwegian language, 'Jøden' ('The Jew') in 1842 and 'Jødinden' ('The Jewess') in 1844, in which he challenged the Christian spirit of his countrymen. 'Jøden' had been distributed to all members of Storting prior to the vote. There was a second vote in 1845 and a third in 1848, still not gaining sufficient majorities. Only in 1851 did the Storting vote with a sufficient majority, by 93 to eight votes, to amend §2, six years after the poet's death. The campaign follows the lobbyists' handbook: gaining support for one's cause by tirelessly pushing the right buttons.

Afterword

Although a well-known public figure in his time, Henrik Wergeland was infamous for picking up fights with anyone. Some 40 years after his passing, the later Nobel laureate for Literature, Bjørnstierne Bjørnson, in his campaigns to gain full Norwegian autonomy from Sweden, polished Wergeland's image. Instead of publicly speaking about Wergeland's unspeakable public behaviour with prostitutes and propensity for fist fights, Bjørnson managed to sanctify the poet as the one who institutionalized the '17 mai-feiring', the celebration of the Constitution that was signed on 17 May 1814. Bjørnson also hailed Wergeland as being a sole civilizing force when lobbying for human rights. He understood that a young nation needs heroes and celebrities. Wergeland, who in the 1880s could no longer fall over drunk, was the perfect hero in Bjørnson's campaign.

References

Bang, T. and Rød, A. (2003) *Informasjon og samfunnskontakt. En innføring* [Information and Public Relations . An Introduction] (Oslo: Abstrakt Forlag).

Warner-Soderholm, G. and Bang, T. (2013) 'The Development of Norwegian PR', *Communication Director*, 2, 38–41.

Bernays, E. L. (1923) *Crystallizing Public Opinion* (New York: Liveright).

Bernays, E. L. (1928) *Propaganda* (New York: Ig Publishing).

Bernays, E. L. (1952) *Public Relations* (Norman: University of Oklahoma Press).

Hertzberg, P. H. (1763 and 1773) *Underretning for Bønder i Norge om den meget nyttige Jord-Frugt Potatos at plante og bruge* [Notification for

DOI: 10.1057/9781137427519.0012

Farmers in Norway about the Planting of Potatoes] (Bergen: Hans Mossins Bogtrykkerie. Det Nyttige Selskab).

Ihlen, Ø. (2013) *PR & strategisk kommunikasjon. Teorier og fagidentitet* [PR and Strategic Communication. Theory and Practice] (Oslo: Universitetsforlaget).

Ihlen, Ø. and Robstad, P. (2004) *Informasjon & samfunnskontakt. Perspektiver og praksis* [Information & Public Relations. Perspectives and Practice] (Bergen: Fagbokforlaget)

DOI: 10.1057/9781137427519.0012

Denmark

Finn Frandsen

The history of PR in Denmark still remains little explored. As in many other European countries, Danish private companies and governmental organizations were involved in various types of public relations activities *ante litteram*, that is before the concept of PR was exported from the US to the Scandinavian countries after World War II. These activities were driven by either commercial or political motives. Denmark once was and, to a certain extent, still is a colonial power, although Greenland and the Faroe Islands today are autonomous countries within the Kingdom of Denmark. However, little is known about how the concepts and practices of PR have been adopted in a Danish context. Apart from Madsen (2000) and a few testimonials delivered by pioneering practitioners 'who were there', no historical studies investigating the development of PR in Denmark have been conducted. Therefore, the following outline focuses on the intellectual and institutional history where there exists some documentation: the early PR literature, the establishment of the first professional association in the 1960s and the first study programme in the 1980s, how the understanding of PR has changed, the creation of the Danish Association of Communication Professionals in 1999, and the 'explosion of the field' after the year 2000.

After World War II: early PR literature

Erhvervslivet og offentligheden: Det amerikanske public relations arbejdet [The Business Community and the Public: US Public Relations Work] (1945), authored by propaganda manager [sic] Poul B. Christensen, is probably the first book on PR written in Danish. PR professionals interested in reading more had to wait more than a decade before a second publication (Petersen, 1956) appeared. The first important handbooks published in Denmark and with the term 'public relations' represented in their titles did not reach the book stores until much later (Blach and Højberg, 1989; Merkelsen, 2010).

Christensen (1945) took a strong commercial perspective on PR in an attempt to locate the new function within the market economy. This perspective was based on the assumption that ultimately every company

DOI: 10.1057/9781137427519.0012

purpose will coincide with an interest in sales. Christensen defined PR as the goodwill policy of a company:

> The purpose of public relations is to avoid or counter an ill-feeling or agitation against a company, a group of companies or business as such, potentially the private capitalist system under which it works, that (a) may lead to regulation or other types of intervention from the public authorities that will limit the freedom of action or the opportunities for profit; (b) reduce sales opportunities directly; or (c) make the work of the companies more complicated. Similarly, the purpose can be to build up goodwill. (p. 123)

Christensen (1945) also claimed that the need for PR was bigger in the US than in Denmark. In Denmark, the workers had their own political party (the Social Democrats); social legislation has created better conditions for the workers; and the trade unions were strong and could negotiate on equal terms with employer associations. Thus, according to the Danish propaganda manager, there was no social, political and economic tension between employees and employers, as in the US, and no serious conflicts between pressure groups and business. In 1945, PR is still an unknown term in a Danish context. However, development started accelerating, especially in two periods during the following 50 years: at the beginning of the 1960s and in the 1980s.

1960s: the first professional association

In 1961, a group of about 20 practitioners established the Danish Public Relations Club (DPRK). The people behind the initiative were divided into two groups: (1) people working for private companies, such as Danish Esso, Danish Shell and Tuborg, who had already established PR functions in their organizations; and (2) journalists. The latter had been excluded from the Danish Union of Journalists (DJ) which at that time did not allow its members to do PR/publicity work. The creation of DPRK was the sign of a new awareness of the importance of the field, especially in the Danish private sector. Public organizations did not join DPRK until the late 1960s.

According to the statutes of DPRK at the time, public relations was defined as 'a continuous and systematic management function by which companies, private and public organizations and institutions seek to achieve understanding, sympathy and support in those parts of the public they have or will get in contact with' (DKF, 2014). By defining PR as a management function, DPRK members wanted to eliminate the negative image of PR professional as 'gin & tonic men' participating in cocktail parties and writing press releases for the news media (Madsen, 2000).

DPRK's first code of ethics, agreed in 1964, set up guidelines for the relationship between professionals themselves and between practitioners and clients. Again, the purpose was to create an understanding and respect for the profession. In 1966, the first PR award was established by DPRK. The young association also published several publications. In 1970, no fewer than three publications appeared, including what DPRK considered to be the first Danish public relations book: *Menings-målinger i PR-arbejdet* [Opinion Polls in pR Work] (Hegedahl, 1970), *Public Relations i samfundsperspektiv* [Public Relations in Society Perspective] (Lindegaard, 1970) and *Kontakt til lokalsamfundet* [Contact with the Local Community] (Schmidt, 1970).

1980s: PR education starts

The 1980s represent another important decade in the development of PR. In 1982, DPRK changed its name to the Danish Public Relations Association (DPRF). In the same year, the International Public Relations Association (IPRA) published its Gold Paper No. 4, 'A Model for Public Relations Education for Professional Practice' (IPRA, 1983) recommending, among other things, that full-time PR education should be offered in universities at the Master's level and that it should be taught as a social science with both academic and professional emphases.

In 1984, inspired by the IPRA Gold Paper, DPRF established an educational committee which produced a proposal for a full-time PR course. Two years later, after a process involving the Directorate for Higher Education in Denmark, the first cohort of full-time students entered Roskilde University.

In 1988, the Danish Association of Public Relations Agencies was established, and today (2015), this trade association counts almost 30 member organizations.

At the end of the decade, Thomas Blach and Jesper Højberg, two practitioners, edited the first important Danish handbook on public relations: *PR: Håndbog i information og public relations* [PR. handbook of information and public relations]. At the end of part 1, a section entitled 'Towards a new understanding of public relations' highlighted their conceptualization of PR as a practice:

> Public relations covers both the relations and the communication between the company and the public ... The overall goal of public relations is to

DOI: 10.1057/9781137427519.0012

contribute to the achievement of the fundamental purposes of the company. These purposes are again based on objectives and values for which public accept can be obtained ... Public relations is based on the correspondence between good behavior and communication with the right arguments and the right profile, at the right time and in the right place ... The company's relations to the public is a manifestation of its actions, and ... you will only have the image you deserve. A reputation cannot be selected .... (Blach and Højberg, 1989, p. 196)

After 2000

In 1999, the Danish Public Relations Association merged with Foreningen af Informationsmedarbejdere i Kommuner, Amter og Staten (FIKAS), and out of this merger came the Danish Association of Communication Professionals (DKF). Today (2015), DKF has almost 3500 members. One outcome of this merger was that the term 'public relations' disappeared from the name of the new association and was replaced by the much broader term 'communication'. Another key term, that is 'professional', also became more frequently used in DKF documentation, including its mission statement: to 'develop and strengthen the professional competencies, identity, and network of the members' and to 'increase and make the value of professional communication more visible' (DKF, 2014).

However, the term 'public relations' is still present in the definition of the association's purpose:

> The purpose of the association is to support and to promote the good use of *communication, information* and *public relations* as a strategic and operational tool in companies, organizations, and the public sector'. (DKF, 2014, our emphasis)

The order of words in this definition is not without reason and tells a story. Until the end of the 1970s, 'public relations' seems to have been the preferred term in Denmark; then, in the 1980s, public relations was replaced by 'information', and later, in the 1990s, information was replaced by 'communication'. This trend has been confirmed by a longitudinal study of Danish job advertisements (Frandsen, 2012).

After 2000, communication has 'exploded' both as a profession (occupation), and as a field of education and research. Today, most universities and business schools in Denmark have study programmes and established research centres, especially within corporate communication.

DOI: 10.1057/9781137427519.0012

122   *Larsåke Larsson, Tor Bang, and Finn Frandsen*

References

Blach, T. and Højberg Christensen, J. (eds) (1989) *PR. Håndbog i information og public relations* [PR. Handbook of Information and Public Relations] (Copenhagen: Borgens Forlag).

Christensen, P. B. (1945) *Erhvervslivet og offentligheden: Det amerikanske public relations arbejdet* [The Business Community and the Public: The US Public Relations Work] (Copenhagen: Einar Harcks Forlag).

DKF – Dansk Kommunikationsforening [Danish Association of Communication Professionals] (2014) 'Home page', http://www. kommunikationsforening.dk, date accessed, 10 November 2014.

Frandsen, F. (2012) 'Looking through a Keyhole: Job Advertisements and the Institutionalization of Strategic Communication in Denmark. a Longitudinal Study (1960–2010)', https://au.academia. edu/FinnFrandsen, date accessed 10 November 2014.

Hegedahl, P. (1970) *Meningsmålinger i PR-arbejdet* [Opinion Polls in PR Work] (Copenhagen: DPRK).

IPRA International Public Relations Association (1983) 'A Model for Public Relations Education for Professional Practice', Gold Paper No. 4 (London: IPRA)

Lindegaard, H. (1970) *Public relations i samfundsperspektiv* [Public Relations in Society Perspective] (Copenhagen: Steen Hasselbalchs Forlag).

Madsen, M. (2000) *Public Relations in Denmark*, unpublished Master's dissertation (University of Stirling, UK).

Merkelsen, H. (ed.) (2010) *Håndbog i strategisk public relations* [Handbook of Strategic Public Relations] (Frederiksberg: Samfundslitteratur).

Petersen, K. (1956) Den åbne dørs politik i erhvervslivet [The Open-Door Policy in the Business World], *Erhvervsøkonomisk Tidsskrift*, 20, 57–65.

Schmidt, J. (1970) *Kontakt til lokalsamfundet* [Contact with the Local Community] (Copenhagen: DPRK).

DOI: 10.1057/9781137427519.0012

9
Spain

Natalia Rodríguez-Salcedo and Jordi Xifra

Abstract: Spain is different. *So said a well-known post-World War II slogan which became popular in tourism advertising in the 1960s. Indeed, the evolution of public relations (PR) in Spain has several distinctive features. As a profession, it began with the opening of the first agency dedicated to offering full PR services in November 1960, during the dictatorship of General Francisco Franco. Despite mild censorship of promotional activities and image campaigns, the profession continued to break ground until the end of Francoism in 1975, when the country became more open and its process towards democracy began.*

Keywords: dictatorship; democracy; Franco; history of public relations; Spain

Watson, Tom (ed.). *Western European Perspectives on the Development of Public Relations: Other Voices*. Basingstoke: Palgrave Macmillan, 2015. DOI: 10.1057/9781137427519.0013.

The historical study of the beginnings of PR in a dictatorship has been hindered by the reality that some early initiatives were forgotten due to their association with propaganda activities and a supposed lack of professionalism (Arceo, J. L., 2006). Some scholars underline the scarcity of research before the 1980s (ibid.). At the moment (2014), there are no books with full coverage of the history of the subject in Spain, although several articles and book chapters have appeared in the previous few years (Arceo, A., 2004; Arceo, J. L., 2006, 2004; Checa, 2007; Gutiérrez and Rodríguez, 2009; Matilla, 2015; Montero, Rodríguez and Verdera, 2010; Moreno, 2002, 2004; Noguero i Grau, 1994, 2004; Rodríguez-Salcedo, 2008, 2010, 2012; Tomás Bravo, 1981, 1983; Xifra, 2012). Therefore this chapter attempts to describe the birth of PR as a profession which, during the dictatorship, challenged Francoist propaganda and censorship, thanks to the personality of some pioneers, and to explain its professional and academic evolution up to the start of the 21st century.

In order to establish a precise timeline, a thorough bibliographical review has been carried out, not only of academic books and journals but also of periodicals, in order to find documentary proof with precise dates. In addition, some of the pioneers, Agustí de Uribe, Teresa Dorn, Francisco Fontcuberta, Jordi Garriga, Joaquín Maestre, Jesús Ulled and Luis Viñas, have been interviewed in depth. The oral sources have been corroborated and complemented by means of two historical archives: that of the first Spanish PR company, now to be found at the University of Navarra, and that of the International Public Relations Association (IPRA) at Bournemouth University. Finally, the chronology of the profession has been broken up into five periods, or stages. These tend to coincide with prominent and developing historical events, either political or economic, but not necessarily resulting in a better conception of the PR profession.

Precedents (1900–1953)

During the first half of the 20th century, there were some isolated initiatives which may be considered the predecessors of PR, both in the entrepreneurial and institutional sectors. Thus, companies established in Spain from varied sectors, such as the food industry, Nestlé (Nestlé Sociedad, 1992) or the perfume industry, *Perfumerías Gal* (Alvarado y De

DOI: 10.1057/9781137427519.0013

Andrés, 1998, 1999), were devoted to the promotion of good relations with customers. Some of these initiatives, in the hands of the master of advertising, Pedro Prat Gaballí, were called 'educational campaigns', as, before publicizing the sales of a toothpaste, for example, they carried out a dental hygiene campaign between 1931 and 1933, initiating people into habits of dental hygiene (Rodríguez-Salcedo, 2008).

In the area of public administration, before the Civil War (1936–1939), there were some outstanding programmes on the subject of tourism and road safety. The history of Spanish tourism became particularly relevant in the communications area with the creation of the Comisión Nacional de Turismo [National Commission for Tourism] (1905–1911), one of the first official tourism organizations in Europe. In the following years, the establishment of the Comisaría Regia de Turismo [Regal Commission for Tourism] (1911–1928) and the Patronato Nacional de Turismo [National Tourism Board] (1928–1936) were to complete this work until the outbreak of the Civil War. These organizations promoted Spain as a national and international tourist destination. On the other hand, towards the end of the 1920s, social campaigns, although few and far between, were carried out to improve road safety (regarding the use of trams) and hygiene, both in Barcelona and in the rest of the country, through the 'Social Hygiene and Propaganda' section of the Dirección General de Sanidad de la República Española [General Directorate of Health of the Spanish Republic]. These programmes ran parallel to entrepreneurial development, although they were far less intense in Spain which was going through a tumultuous period that resulted in a Civil War.

The end of the Civil War was accompanied by the need to reorganize and reconstruct Spain under the dictatorial regime of General Franco (1939–1975); the situation was exacerbated by a world war. Therefore, the political and historical circumstances of the country between 1939 and 1945 brought about state intervention and control of economic activity. A rigid economy of rationing took precedence, with no possibility of exchange with foreign countries. Moreover there was a drop in productivity and, consequently, a fall in income per capita (Clavera et al., 1973). With little consumption or production the country came to an economic standstill.

After the end of the world war in 1945, Spain remained isolated from the exterior, a 'marginal zone' (ibid.) outside the European Recovery Plan (the Marshall Plan) which helped to finance European reconstruction.

DOI: 10.1057/9781137427519.0013

The delicate political situation led the Franco regime to renew the regime's cabinet in an attempt to present political changes in a more positive light. The economic difficulties of the country continued until the 1950s.

It is in these years that a series of posters with advice on the eradication of epidemics and diseases, in line with the actions already carried out by the public administration in the 1930s can be found. In these difficult years, the Francoist State was concerned with reduction of infant mortality, which had been present in the country since the beginning of the century but had been intensified by the Civil War. With the highest rates in Europe, the Ministry for Governance, through its General Directorate for Health and 'Propaganda Section', published posters offering advice to mothers and providing guidance on child healthcare. In the absence of a detailed study of PR in the Franco administration, this example may be considered a precedent.

However, it was in the 1950s that two entrepreneurial initiatives appeared and signalled the birth of the profession. On one hand, the Catalonian advertising agent Joan Fontcuberta, at the Danis agency (Barcelona) developed a 'prestige advertising' campaign for its client Mistol, a dishwashing liquid, with the objective of promoting improvement in human and social relations (Fontcuberta, 1998, p. 177). So, from October 1955 until January 1956, weekly advertisements were published in the press advising the Spanish people to be better, to look after their parents, to give up their seats on the bus, to respond with a smile and so on. On the other hand, Juan Viñas, a radio journalist, had since 1957 been working on the Crusade for Ocular Protection, a campaign promoted by Industrias de Ópticas (INDO). The opticians company had been set up in 1940 by the Cottet brothers, who were from France. Encouraged by similar initiatives in France and Great Britain, the campaign went on for 25 years. The Crusade did not merely intend to contribute to better vision for Spaniards, but also proposed to make the public aware of the necessity of caring for their eyes (Viñas, 2003).

Thus there had been campaigns in Spain since the 1930s which nowadays would be considered as PR. Prat Gaballí and Fontcuberta worked in the Spanish advertising industry and developed PR programmes, although they called them 'educational advertising' (1931–1933) or 'prestige advertising' (1955–1958), respectively. It was Prat Gaballí who first used the term 'public relations' in Spain (Reina and González, 2014; Rodríguez-Salcedo, 2008, 2010). In his book *Publicidad Combativa*

DOI: 10.1057/9781137427519.0013

[Combative Advertising] (1953), he translated the American term as 'general relations' and considered that it was different from advertising, although it worked in the same way: 'it includes relations with the public, public entities, or individuals from one's own organization, which a company may have in order to increase its esteem and likeability' (Prat Gaballí, 1953, p. 449). This definition was, however, ignored by the professionals of the times.

1960s: the first agency, association movements and PR higher education college

The term 'public relations' was not, however, applied to professional practice until 1958, when Joaquín Maestre, an enquiring young man who had been working for the advertising agency Danis for a little over two years, travelled to Brussels to attend a Congress and to translate for Fontcuberta, his boss and friend. While waiting in the hall of the hotel he was staying in, by chance he began a conversation with one of the pioneers of European PR, Lucien Matrat (Gutiérrez and Rodríguez, 2009; Rodríguez-Salcedo 2010). At the end of the conversation, young Maestre realized that the campaigns that his agency had carried out in Spain and labelled 'prestige advertising' were referred to as 'public relations' in the rest of Europe and the United States (Joaquín Maestre, personal communication, 1999, 2003). His interest in this new discipline soon produced results and, two years after his return to Spain and having read books in English on PR, he opened his own consultancy.

S.A.E. de RP [Spanish Public Relations Limited Company], the first company offering PR services, was founded in Barcelona by Joaquín Maestre and the journalist Juan Viñas in November 1960. Maestre's initiative and youth undoubtedly benefited from the political and economic situation. After the end of the total international boycott, the government could no longer blame its low economic capacity on causes outside the regime (Harrison, 1998). On the verge of a terrible economic crisis, the 1950s ended with a Government Decree which reorganized the central administration and created the Office for Economic Coordination and Programming, which was to give cohesion to the economic measures of different ministries, and to prepare a joint perspective for the economic development plans. Finally, in February 1962, the Commission for Social and Economic Development Planning was created and settled on

DOI: 10.1057/9781137427519.0013

three consecutive Social and Economic Development Plans: 1964–1967, 1968–1971 and 1972–1975.

The second PR company was begun, also in Barcelona, in 1964 by Jesús Ulled. He and his partner Víctor Sagi created Ulled & Sagi (Balsebre, 2011). Sagi contributed a small portfolio of regular clients. Shortly afterwards (1965), they agreed to dissolve this partnership; Sagi then became one of Ulled's regular clients and the latter opened the doors of his own business 'Jesús Ulled. Asesor de Relaciones Públicas' [Jesús Ulled. Public Relations Consultant].

As had occurred in Europe, and on the contrary to the United States, the first attempts to institutionalize the profession happened quickly. Particularly relevant was this similarity with Europe that occurred in a country and at a time when the social structure had no corporate tradition. This deficiency was due in part to the Civil War and the years of dictatorship, which did not promote civic associations outside the Francoist programme. However, this opposition to professional association may have contributed to the failure in the medium to long term for this type of organisation amongst PR practitioners in the two main cities, Barcelona and Madrid.

While in Barcelona, a city on the Mediterranean Sea and close to the frontier with France, the earliest consultancies were appearing, the first PR professionals in the capital Madrid, who had their roots in technical positions in the public administration, began to promote associationism. Shortly after the opening of the first agency, the first association movement began with the creation of the Asociación Técnica de Relaciones Públicas [Public Relations Technical Association] in 1961, which lasted barely two years (Maestre, personal communication).

In 1962, the first Spanish journal devoted entirely to the profession, *Relaciones Públicas* [Public Relations] edited by Fernando Lozano, was published. Despite the irregularity of its issues, it covered the main events and campaigns of the period, as it included articles by European and American academics.

Maestre was the first Spanish PR agent to be recognized by an international association, IPRA, in 1963. In the same decade he was followed by others, such as Rafael Ansón (from 1967), Esteban Bassols (1967), José María Laffitte (1967), Fernando Díaz de San Pedro (1968), Manuel Ortiz Sánchez (1968), José M. Rico (1968) and the Rev. Carlos Tomás Bravo (1968).

After the collapse of the first association in 1965, professionals in Madrid created the Centro Español de Relaciones Públicas [Spanish

DOI: 10.1057/9781137427519.0013

Centre for PR] (CENERP), and those from Barcelona, the Agrupación Española de RP [Spanish Association of PR] (AERP). At this time, the industrial take-off after the launch of the First Development Plan was intended to achieve major growth of the economy, but the period between 1966 and 1969 turned out to be bitter-sweet for PR. On one hand, in 1966, the year that the Press Law relaxed the earlier Francoist censorship, Maestre convinced the IPRA to hold its General Assembly in Barcelona in May to grant recognition to the PR profession in Spain. The only condition the IPRA insisted on was that there should be one single association. Therefore, the two associations joined together with the generic title, Spanish Centre for PR. Along with this, there was the joint celebration of the First Spanish PR Congress. However, the apparent agreement between the Barcelona and Madrid chapters was compromised and, in 1967, they went their separate ways. In the face of this new breakdown, the AERP in Barcelona made a comeback, with the intention of promoting an educational project for the establishment of the Escuela Superior de Relaciones Públicas [PR Higher Education College], which, under the presidency of Jorge Xifra Heras, opened in 1968.

In brief, the 1960s was notable for attempted associationism and the search for professional recognition, together with the establishment of the first educational programmes. Life in a dictatorship did not hinder the speedy development of the profession during those years. All the pioneers consulted agreed that the regime's censorship did not interfere with their profession. The tacit agreement simply meant that they did not interfere in politics.

1969–1975: attempts to shape a legal framework

Notwithstanding the problems stemming from the lack of agreement on a single association, the 1960s closed with a joint achievement for the professionals in Madrid and Barcelona: the organization of the First Annual PR Assembly in 1969, whose objective was to work for institutional recognition of PR. The participants made a real effort to combine their interests and produced a draft bill to recognize PR as a profession. It was presented to the Cortes [Parliament] by the Minister for Information and Tourism in April 1971, but was not accepted by Ministers as they did not believe PR to be 'mature' enough.

DOI: 10.1057/9781137427519.0013

Despite this disappointment, Francoism, which had been living on borrowed time due to the caudillo's poor state of health, departed but left some partial achievements for the profession. In 1973, the Agrupación Sindical Nacional de Técnicos en Relaciones Públicas [National Union of PR Technicians] was created. Along the same lines of effective legal recognition for the profession, a Ministerial Order was published on 14 September 1974, which provisionally sanctioned the curriculum for the School of Communication Sciences and included a degree in Advertising and Public Relations, as an extension of the earlier degree in Advertising. The provisional curriculum for all Schools of Communication Sciences at Spanish universities allowed for the existence of three sections in the second cycle: journalism, audiovisual sciences, advertising and PR, which would not come into force until 1992. Second, two new Orders regulated the creation of the Official Register of PR Technicians and an official list of professionals (Noguero i Grau, 1994).

1975–1990s: development of practice and education curricula in democracy

From 1975 onwards, the democratic process in Spain wrought many political, social and economic changes. As such, it marked a turning point in the communication market, which saw a dramatic rise in both the supply and demand of information (Gutiérrez and Rodríguez, 2009). The increase in the number of communication services as a result of the implementation of freedom of the press (Barrera, 1995) acted as an incentive for public and private organizations.

After the dictatorship of Franco, the evolution of Spanish PR split into two periods (Gutiérrez and Rodríguez, 2009): the development under the democratic system (1975–1989) and the recognition of PR as strategic value (1990–to the present).

Economic growth was accompanied by increased investment in advertising and other areas, including marketing and non-commercial communications. The public and private sectors needed corporate communication as managerial function, and this could be contracted through agencies or consultancies or created through internal structures with qualified professionals. The demand for this type of service explains why international PR consultancies opened their first offices during the 1980s (Gutiérrez and Rodríguez, 2009).

DOI: 10.1057/9781137427519.0013

The main factor for the development of PR industry was the recognition by the new democratic constitution (1978) of the freedom of speech and the right of access to the media. The Supreme Court of Spain has stated that the freedom of speech contains a mandate awarding important social and political groups the right to demand that nothing be done to impede free speech. Therefore, the first democratic elections (1977), the approval of a new democratic constitution (1978), the acceptance of Spain in the Common Market in 1986, the Universal Exposition of Seville and the Barcelona Olympics, both in 1992, boosted the market for PR.

As Josephs and Josephs (1992) stated, 'during the days of Francisco Franco, practicing PR in Spain was arguably something of a contradiction, with practitioners faced with tremendous problems in getting coverage for private sector companies' (p. 18). Nevertheless, the new political context was the ideal field for the growth of media relations as one of the key practices of PR and for getting media coverage. Yet, the exact size of the PR practice in Spain was unclear, though every sign demonstrated a very extensive growth, particularly since the mid-1980s. Virtually all firms reported fee volume up by 10 to 20 per cent or more in 1991, and some expected to do even better in 1992 (Josephs and Josephs, 1992). Indeed, 1992 was a key date for the history of Spain, the history of its economy and, by extension, the history of corporate communications.

In this decade, two new Spanish professional associations were created: Asociación de Empresas Consultoras en Relaciones Públicas y Comunicación, ADECEC [Association of PR and Communication Consultants] and Asociación de Directivos de Comunicación, DIRCOM [Association of Communication Directors]. ADECEC was formed in 1991 by representatives of the PR consultancies with the highest turnovers. It currently (2014) comprises 32 firms, and it is Spanish industry's most important PR employer organization. DIRCOM was founded in 1992 and includes the positioning of communication as a strategic tool for organizational management among its goals.

As Josephs and Josephs (1992) argued, this situation was in contrast to earlier periods, when the annual growth ran from 25 per cent to 30 per cent. This growth was largely due to the profession's relatively small base after a stable Socialist government was elected in 1982. However, the high growth rate slowed despite the number of events taking place in Spain in 1992. 'Ironically, many consultancies did not want to get too involved in these events other than serving participating clients, according to those interviewed. They felt the up-tick in business would be followed by a letdown' (Josephs and Josephs, 1992, p. 19).

With regard to PR firms, the growth was paralleled by internal departments. As Gutiérrez and Rodríguez (2009) argued, since customers identified communication needs and created own communication structures, they also relied on PR and communications firms. In Spain, throughout the 20th century, the advertising and marketing communication services had increasingly gained importance, especially in terms of investment. From the 1980s, these services were supported and complemented by PR consultancies. Since 1980, the year in which Teresa Dorn opened the first international PR office in Madrid for Burson-Marsteller, the industry has experienced a steady growth, particularly between 1996 and 2008 (Gutiérrez and Rodríguez, 2009).

The 1990s also represented the consolidation of PR education. A new degree in Advertising and PR was recognized as one of the undergraduate programmes offered by Spanish universities. In August 1991, the Ministry of Education and Science (MEC) authorized a degree in Publicidad y Relaciones Públicas [Advertising and PR] (Xifra and Castillo, 2006). This new regulation had important implications for PR education, because the law that ruled the universities established compulsory courses for each undergraduate programme. Recent studies suggest the application of the EU's Bologna process has not helped to strengthen PR contents in the curricula of communication degrees. Only one-fifth of the number of credits is fully devoted to specific PR courses (Moreno, Carrasco and Saperas, 2014). Not surprisingly, several postgraduate programmes on corporate communication and PR have been introduced and have successfully produced graduates who have not undertaken undergraduate studies in PR. They were established, with success, to cover the lack of PR curricula in undergraduate programmes.

Another consequence of the growth of PR on higher education is that this period was also very fruitful in doctoral research compared with previous periods. As Xifra and Castillo (2006) pointed out, the period from 1995 to 2004 witnessed the highest increase in research dissertations: 37 PhD (60 per cent of those presented in the 50-year period from 1956 to 2006). This indicates that there was considerable increase in research into PR and organizational communication over those years, in proportion with the increase in the number of universities offering degrees in Advertising and PR.

DOI: 10.1057/9781137427519.0013

A new century

In terms of recent history of PR, the new century has been characterized by having data gathered in surveys about the profession and the rise of research in PR. ADECEC has been primarily responsible for the first feature and others more recently (Torres and Carrera, 2014). ADECEC published two reports, in 2004 and 2008, which offered a snapshot of a growing PR industry in Spain for the first time. Those were, however, not the first formal studies carried out by this association. As Tilson and Saura (2003) pointed out, the growth of PR consultancy in Spain had been reflected in ADECEC's annual ranking studies. In 2001, ADECEC reported that its total membership billings for 2000 were 58.3 million euros, a 30.7 per cent increase compared with the previous year. Furthermore, total billings for 1999 represented a 27.5 per cent increase over 1998. The top five firms in billings for 2000 were: Burson-Marsteller (arrived 1980), Weber Shandwick Ibérica (1990), Grupo Sanchis Comunicación (1983), J. A. Llorente & O. Cuenca (1995), and Grupo Comunicación Empresarial (1986). Those authors also mentioned a study of strategic communication consultancy by Inforpress, conducted in 2000, which reported that 56 per cent of companies surveyed considered media relations 'very important', and 92 per cent said they had a director of communication (Tilson and Saura, 2003).

Nevertheless, the ADECEC studies, conducted in 2004 and 2008, have presented the most accurate picture of PR practice in the first decade of the new century. According to the 2008 ADECEC report, conducted by the market research firm Sigma Dos and based on interviews with 207 PR practitioners (102 with communication managers at the main Spanish organizations in all industries and 105 with managers and employees of PR firms), the activity carried out by most PR firms was media relations (96 per cent), followed by corporate communication (90.5 per cent). The companies further reported that corporate communication (91 per cent) and internal communication (88 per cent) were the most important functions of their communication departments, followed by media relations (86 per cent) and public affairs (84 per cent). Some 68 per cent considered communication to be a strategic factor in their operations (87 per cent conducted corporate communication programmes), and 89 per cent evaluated the results of these programmes and their corporate image. Those results support the prior argument of Tilson and Saura (2003): 'given the dynamic media environment and

DOI: 10.1057/9781137427519.0013

growing consumerism in Spain, media relations and corporate identity have assumed greater importance' (p. 132). When headquarters locations of the top 30 consultancies are considered, Madrid takes the lead with 67 per cent and Barcelona keeps a modest second place at 27 per cent (Torres and Carrera, 2014).

The early years of the 21st century also represented the growth of academic research for PR. This rise led into the creation of the first association for researchers: Asociación de Investigadores en Relaciones Públicas [Association of Researchers in PR] (AIRP) in 2004. AIRP organizes an annual national conference for Spanish and Latin-American PR scholars. The state of research is one of the most notable landmarks of Spanish PR education and scholarship in the new century due to the internationalization of papers and conference presentations. Today, Spain is the fourth country in the ranking of authors who have published articles in *Public Relations Review*, the leading international academic journal. These data were inconceivable 15 years ago and prove the influence of Spanish scholars on both PR research and the practice.

Conclusion

The purpose of this chapter has been to provide an overview of the development of PR in the course of almost 60 years, and to furnish an analysis of the factors that have shaped practice. The birth and evolution of Spanish PR cannot be understood without its historical context. Although there were some activities that could be considered as precedents of PR in the early years of the 20th century before the Civil War, it was not until the 1950s that the term 'public relations' came into existence. The emerging communication needs of 1950s' society were acutely identified by a group of advertising agents, before undergoing dramatic expansion through the consultancy work of the very few PR companies in existence in Spain during the late-Franco period. Professional agents such as Maestre, who discerned the emerging need and foresaw the subsequent market demand, put in place a network of international contacts and creativity which enabled them to promote the practice, organize it as a profession and coordinate interests as long as they did not interfere with the politics of a dictatorship. With the advent of democracy, PR expanded thanks to a new constitution, democratic elections, international recognition and macro-events in the country.

DOI: 10.1057/9781137427519.0013

Indeed, political, economic, social and media realities in Spain shaped the course of the PR profession.

References

ADECEC (2005) *La comunicación y las relaciones públicas. Radiografía del sector 2004. Las consultoras de comunicación. Las empresas* [Communication and PR. An X-ray of 2004. Communication Consultancies. Organizations] (Madrid: ADECEC).

ADECEC and Sigma Dos (2008) 'La comunicación y las relaciones públicas en España. Radiografía de un sector 2008' [Communication and PR in Spain. An X-ray of 2008] http://www.prnoticias.com/images/stories/comunicacion/ARCHIVOS/presentacin_del_estudio_adecec.pdf, date accessed, 1 October 2014.

Alvarado López, M. C. and De Andrés del Campo, S. (1998) 'Gal: Un siglo de perfumería, un siglo de publicidad' [Gal: A Century of Perfume Industry, a Century of Advertising], *Publifilia: Revista de Culturas Publicitarias*, 1, 23–49.

Alvarado López, M. C. and De Andrés del Campo, S. (1999) 'Gal: Un siglo de perfumería, un siglo de publicidad' [Gal: A Century of Perfume Industry, a Century of Advertising], *Publifilia. Revista de Culturas Publicitarias*, 2, 49–64.

Arceo Vacas, A. (2004) 'Public Relations in Spain: An Introduction', *Public Relations Review*, 30(3), 293–302.

Arceo Vacas, J. L. (2006) 'La investigación de relaciones públicas en España' [Research in Spanish Public Relations], *Anàlisi*, 34, 111–124.

Arceo Vacas, J. L. (ed.) (2004) *Las relaciones públicas en España* [Public Relations in Spain]. (Madrid: McGraw Hill).

Balsebre, A. (2011) *Víctor Sagi. Historia de la Publicidad* [Víctor Sagi. A History of Advertising] (Barcelona: Ediciones Invisibles).

Barrera, C. (1995) *Sin mordaza. Veinte años de prensa en democracia* [Ungagged. Twenty years of Press under Democracy] (Madrid: Temas de Hoy).

Checa, A. (2007) 'Historia de las RRPP' [History of PR], in A. Checa, *Historia de la Publicidad* [History of Advertising] (La Coruña: Netbiblo).

Clavera, J., Esteban, J., Monés, M. A., Montserrat, A. and Ros Hombravella, J. (1973) *Capitalismo español: de la autarquía a la estabilización (1939–1959)* [Spanish Capitalism: From Autarchy to

DOI: 10.1057/9781137427519.0013

Stabilization (1939–1959)], volume 1 (Madrid: Editorial Cuadernos para el Diálogo).

Fontcuberta Vernet, J. (1998) *Hora Cero* [Zero-Hour] (Barcelona: Editorial Thassàlia).

Gutiérrez, E. and Rodríguez, N. (2009) 'Cincuenta años de Relaciones Públicas en España. De la propaganda y la publicidad a la gestión de la reputación' [Fifty Years of Public Relations in Spain. from Propaganda and Advertising to Reputation Management], *Doxa Comunicación*, 9, 13–33.

Harrison, J. (1998) *La economía española: De la Guerra Civil a la Comunidad Europea* [The Spanish Economy: From the Civil War to the European Community] (Madrid: Ediciones Istmo).

Josephs, R. and Josephs, J. W. (1992) 'Spain Gains World Attention as Public Relations Comes of Age', *Public Relations Journal*, 48(5), 18–22.

Matilla, K. (ed.) (2015) *Historia de la comunicación corporativa en Cataluña* [The History of Corporate Communications in Catalonia] (Barcelona: UOC, colección Dircom), in print.

Montero, M., Rodríguez, N. and Verdera, F. (eds) (2010) *Historia de la Publicidad y de las Relaciones Públicas en España (volumen 1). De la nada al consumo. Desde los orígenes hasta 1960* [History of Advertising and Public Relations in Spain (volume 1). From Scratch to Consumption. From the Origins to 1960] (Zamora: Comunicación Social).

Moreno, M. A. (2002) 'Public Relations in Spain in 2002: Antecedents, Present Situations and Future Tendencies', in D. Verčič, B. van Ruler, I. Jensen, D. Moss and J. White (eds) *The Status of Public Relations Knowledge in Europe and Around the World* (Bled: Pristop Communication).

Moreno, M. A. (2004) 'Spain', in B. van Ruler and D. Verčič (eds) *Public Relations and Communication Management in Europe: A Nation-by-Nation Introduction to Public Relations Theory and Practice* (Berlin: Mouton de Gruyter).

Moreno, M. A., Carrasco A. and Saperas, E. (2014) 'Los efectos del proceso Bolonia en el currículum de las Relaciones Públicas. Análisis del estado de la cuestión' [The Effects of the Bologna Process on the Curricula of Public Relations. A Critical State of the Art], *Sphera Publica*, June, 163–184.

Nestlé Sociedad (1992) *Una historia de la publicidad española: Reflejos de más de un siglo de Nestlé* [A History of Spanish Advertising: Reflections of More Than a Century with Nestlé]. (Barcelona: AEPA).

DOI: 10.1057/9781137427519.0013

Noguero i Grau, A. (1994) 'La historia de las relaciones públicas en España: 1954–1990' [The History of Public Relations in Spain: 1954–1990], *Revista Universitaria de Publicidad y Relaciones Públicas*, 1, 67–90.

Noguero i Grau, A. (2004) 'Principales acontecimientos en la evolución de las relaciones públicas en España' [Landmarks in the Evolution of Public Relations in Spain] in J. L. Arceo Vacas (ed.) *Las relaciones públicas en España* [Public Relations in Spain] (Madrid: McGraw-Hill).

Prat Gaballí, P. (1953) *Publicidad Combativa* [Combative Advertising] (Barcelona: Editorial Labor).

Reina Estévez, J. and González España, M. I. (2014) 'Prat Gaballí y Juan Beneyto: una aproximación a la introducción de la disciplina de las relaciones públicas en España' [Prat Gaballí and Juan Beneyto: An Approach to the Introduction of the Public Relations Discipline in Spain], *Revista Internacional de Relaciones Públicas*, 4(7), 177–196.

Rodríguez-Salcedo, N. (2008) 'Public Relations before "Public Relations" in Spain: An Early History (1881–1960)', *Journal of Communication Management*, 12(4), 279–293.

Rodríguez-Salcedo, N. (2010) 'Relaciones Públicas en Dictadura: el inicio de la profesión en España (1960–1975)' [Public Relations under a Dictatorship: The Beginning of the Profession in Spain (1960–1975)], in M. Montero, N. Rodríguez, J. Rodríguez, and J. del Río (eds) *Historia de la Publicidad y de las Relaciones Públicas en España (volumen 2). La edad de oro de la comunicación comercial. Desde 1960 hasta 2000* [History of Advertising and Public Relations in Spain (volume 2). The Golden Age of Commercial Communications. From 1960 to 2000] (Zamora: Comunicación Social).

Rodríguez-Salcedo, N. (2012) 'Mapping Public Relations in Europe: Writing National Histories against the US Paradigm', *Comunicación y Sociedad*, 25 (2), 331–374.

Tilson, D. J. and Saura, P. (2003) 'Public Relations and the New Golden Age of Spain: A Confluence of Democracy, Economic Development and the Media', *Public Relations Review*, 29, 125–143.

Tomás Bravo, C. M. (1981) 'Las Relaciones Públicas en España' [Public Relations in Spain], in P. Lesly (ed.) *Nuevo Manual de Relaciones Públicas* [New Handbook of Public Relations] volume 2 (Barcelona: Editorial Martínez Roca).

Tomás Bravo, C. M. (1983) 'Las Relaciones Públicas en España' [Public Relations in Spain], in C. Lougovoy and M. Linon, *Relaciones*

DOI: 10.1057/9781137427519.0013

Públicas: función de gobierno de la empresa y de la administración
[Public Relations: Governance Function for Organizations and
Administration] (Barcelona: Editorial Hispano Europea).

Torres and Carrera (2014) *PR Noticias Informe PR. España 2014* [Report
on PR. Spain 2014], http://torresycarrera.com/files/Informes/
Informe-PR-Spain-2014.pdf, date accessed 1 October 2014.

Viñas Rexach, F. (2003) *El goig de viure. Joan Viñas Bona* [The Joy of
Living] (Barcelona: Editorial Edimurtra).

Xifra, J. (2012) 'On Decrees, Disputes and Definitions', *Communication
Director*, April, 40–43.

Xifra, J. and Castillo, A. (2006) 'Forty Years of Doctoral Public Relations
Research in Spain: A Quantitative Study of Dissertation Contribution
to Theory Development', *Public Relations Review*, 32, 302–308.

DOI: 10.1057/9781137427519.0013

10
United Kingdom

Jacquie L'Etang

Abstract: *The chapter distinguishes between occupational and societal approaches to British public relations (PR) history and reviews a range of literature that explores socio-cultural, religious and political influences. Reference is made to international and national political change (conflict, colonialism, decolonization), and its effects on the communications of politicians, policy-makers and government administrators in a democratic context. Attention is paid to the diffusion of communications practices in corporate contexts, such as utilities, and increased business awareness of the importance of political lobbying. The formation of a professional body in 1948 is noted, along with some discussion of its ambition for professional status for the occupation in the face of critical opposition from journalists.*

Keywords: education; professional project; professionalism, professionalization; propaganda; 'proto-public relations'

Watson, Tom (ed.). *Western European Perspectives on the Development of Public Relations: Other Voices.* Basingstoke: Palgrave Macmillan, 2015. DOI: 10.1057/9781137427519.0014.

This chapter focuses on the emergence of public relations (PR) as a distinct, named occupation in the 20th century. This excludes centuries of political and public communication, religious 'devotional–promotional' communication, nationalism, advocacy and activism. Yet if PR is understood as taking place 'at points of organizational or societal change ... cluster[ing] around (1) public policy formation; (2) organizational change and development (3) public issues such as the environment (4) major global shifts such as war or global financial collapse' (L'Etang, 2011, p. 224), then it quickly becomes apparent that a vast range of critical incidents, protest and social movements may legitimately fall within the ambit of PR history.

To give a few examples of promotional activities that some would describe as 'proto-public relations': ancient monuments and heritage sites have been and remain symbolically important over time for different tribes and publics, invested in meaning and re-invented meanings and used to articulate collective identities, traditions and affiliations; conflict, conquest, colonization over power and resources require supporters and networks (the rise and fall of Mercia, the rise of Wessex, Wars of the Roses, England, Bonnie Prince Charlie, Scotland); migrations (17th-century promotional work to tempt East Anglican emigration to New England); public health communications (the Bubonic Plague or 'Black Death' in mid-14th century, prevention of diphtheria in early 20th century, the promotion of the 'modern cremation movement' (Kazmier, 2009)); social reform, democratization, civil rights (universal suffrage, women's rights, penal reform, Quaker business philanthropy – the latter being part of the history of corporate social responsibility (L'Etang, 1994)).

Conceiving public communication and intra-cultural communication as the antecedents of contemporary PR positions the occupation as central to societal dynamics, part of the fabric of cultural exchange and contest. Such an interpretation may challenge technological determinism or ideologically driven accounts that position PR as necessarily capitalist, even if its role in the establishment and promotion of neo-liberalism is taken-for-granted in some quarters (Miller and Dinan, 2008; Dinan and Miller, 2007; Logan, 2014). A societal approach also repositions historical PR beyond the field's literature to broader histories that take political, economic and socio-cultural change as their focus.

In this chapter key themes and structural determinants that seem significant in the emergence of the PR occupation in the British Isles are outlined, drawing on 67 oral histories, archives and published literature.

DOI: 10.1057/9781137427519.0014

Historical literature on British PR

There is a modest amount of 'proto-history' within British PR historical literature, exemplified by Norris (2002) who explored the instructional communications of English monarchs in the modern era (1500–1800). Subsequently, Watson explored the cult of Saint Swithun, as part of a campaign to reform the Anglo-Saxon church to a more rigorous monastic style and to provide a focus for pilgrimage (Watson, 2008). Watson's approach was adopted by Croft, Hartland and Skinner (2008) in their analysis of rumours, legends and myths concerning Glastonbury Abbey in the medieval period.

Moore (2014) took a broader European approach in analyzing the public and political communication of rulers in the post-Roman Early Medieval period where, 'The media once available to Rome...had collapsed with the buildings. Gone were the state-mandated rituals, statuary, imperial cults, control over the calendar, and widespread correspondence in one or two languages...the organizations that managed communications on behalf of the state – the officially sanctioned official religion, the army, the local and central bureaucracy, and the emperor himself – were also overthrown' (p. 130).

Histories focusing more narrowly on the PR occupation have explored its professionalization in the context of 20th-century Britain, including the emergence and development of education (L'Etang, 1998, 1999b, 2004; L'Etang and Pieczka, 1996; Pieczka and L'Etang, 2001, 2006) and its gendered nature (Yaxley, 2013; L'Etang, 2015a in press). Although these works drew on interviews of oral history and the archive of the (Chartered) Institute of Public Relations ((C)IPR), they incorporated both an urban and a regional bias, tending to privilege accounts from London and the South-East as a large number of practitioners from the earlier eras were located there.

Conference papers on British history presented at the International History of Public Relations Conference (IHPRC) have included a number of themes. For example, professionalization and education have been of interest: Berendt (2010) analyzed early curricula at Bournemouth University; Garsten and Howard (2011) explored the evolution of UK PR consultancies during 1985–2010; Bailey and Laville (2011) examined the emergence of PR education in the UK; Watson explored the historical challenges of PR evaluation (Watson, 2011).

Politics, public affairs and propaganda have been of interest to others, including Gregory's (2011) discussion of the emergence of government

DOI: 10.1057/9781137427519.0014

communication practices from 1854 (2011); McGrath's analysis of the UK's 'first parliamentary lobbyist', Charles Weller Kent 1913–1927 (McGrath, 2010) and his exploration of the use of the terms 'lobbying' and 'lobbyist' in parliamentary and journalism sources (ibid., 2011); research that explores the historical tensions and politics regarding the constitution and varied cultural and national identities of the 'United Kingdom' and its consequences (Rice and Somerville, 2013; Somerville and Kirby, 2013). These analyses show how much potential there is for PR historians to offer a variety of perspectives both at the proto-level and the narrower occupational–professional level on British historical experiences at national, regional and local levels.

Government propaganda

The merged identities of public communication, intelligence, propaganda and PR are most apparent in the context of wartime propaganda. In 1914, Charles Masterman, former journalist and Cabinet member became head of the War Propaganda Bureau that conducted international media relations and wrote, produced and distributed a range of persuasive communications (Kunczik, 2014, pp. 92–93) primarily directed at attracting US support for the war effort. Masterman was also a significant influence on one of the early British PR consultants, Alan Campbell-Johnson (Lord Mountbatten's press attaché 1947–1948) who co-established Johnson-Crosse in 1946, held accounts for Esso, Procter and Gamble, Gillette and Coca Cola and was a long-term associate of Hill & Knowlton, as well as President of the IPR 1956–1957 (L'Etang, 2004, pp. 30–31, 105–106).

After three years of conflict, the Americans finally entered the war in 1917 and a Department of Enemy Propaganda was formed under one press baron, Lord Northcliffe, while the Ministry of Information (MoI) was formed under another press baron, Lord Beaverbrook, thus establishing the pattern and practices of revolving doors between propaganda/PR, journalism and politics which remain a feature in the British Isles. The Ministry of Information was not re-opened until the beginning of World War II in 1939 employing increasing numbers of communications specialists. The British Broadcasting Corporation (BBC) was central to British propaganda, maintaining the trust of the British public and a reputation overseas for 'an honest, free and truthful media, yet which

DOI: 10.1057/9781137427519.0014

gave practically nothing away to an ever-vigilant enemy' (Pronay, 1982, p. 174 cited in L'Etang, 2004, p. 44). Subversive activities were carried out under the auspices of the Special Operations Executive (SOE) and Political Warfare Executive (PWE) (L'Etang, 2004, pp. 42–44). Head of SOE's French section was Colonel Maurice Buckmaster who had worked for Ford prior to the war, and post-war became director of Ford's PR in the UK, later still doing freelance and representing the French champagne industry (ibid., p. 48). He was a significant figure in British PR and President (1955–1956) of the IPR and was one of many whose careers seamlessly encompassed propaganda, intelligence and civilian PR, a telling pattern. Throughout the 20th century those with designated responsibilities for various forms of information management moved between government and corporate environments, for example Basil Clarke held pre-Great War posts at the *Daily Mail*, Special Intelligence at the Ministry of Reconstruction, post-war posts at Ministry of Health and the Director of Public Information at Dublin Castle (Grant, cited in L'Etang, 2004, p. 93; Evans, 2013). Of the latter post Miller and Dinan commented,

> [Clarke] directed the British propaganda operation against the Irish republican movement ... in this role [he] developed his ideas and tactics on 'propaganda by news'. The key quality of the propaganda was 'verisimilitude' – having an air of truth ... the British policy was to disseminate lies and half-truths which gave the appearance of truth. (Miller and Dinan, 2008, p. 16)

In 1924, Clarke set up Editorial Services which his son described as the first PR consultancy and it continued into the 1960s (L'Etang, 2004, p. 54). Clarke's son claimed his father had strong Atlantic connections and that 'jointly with his friend Ivy Lee of America he coined the phrase "public relations" and began to use it about the same time (1924) (Clarke, 1969, p. 9 cited in L'Etang, 2004, p. 53). However, Ivy Lee Jr wrote, 'I don't remember ever having heard of him [Basil Clarke] ... neither my brother nor I have recollection of my father having contact with any British practitioners' (personal correspondence, 1998; L'Etang, 2004, p. 54).

The emergence of political communication comprised a number of discrete categories: the practice of external (international) and internal (domestic) propaganda during times of conflict (as outlined above); central government information directed at the populace in relation to policy or behavioural advice (health and safety campaigns); local government information campaigns in relation to policy-in-practice and citizen education and guidance (especially important during post-

DOI: 10.1057/9781137427519.0014

war reconstruction); political communication as practised by political parties. An important distinctive feature in the United Kingdom was the separation of civil servants (the cadre of bureaucrats responsible for the development of policy options and administration of policy choices made by politicians) from party politics. In the first part of the 20th century, civil servants responsible for communication at local and national levels were integrated into specialist ministries, and it was not until 1946, when the Ministry of Information was disbanded, that the Central Office of Information (COI) was formed. This became the government's marketing and communications agency until 2011 when it was dissolved following budget cuts and the rump of its activities transferred to the Cabinet Office. PR and marketing expertise became increasingly central to various government policies, for example the nationalization and denationalization of key industries.

The civil service was conceived as a neutral body of advisers whose careers might encompass a variety of political administrations without compromising their career progression or seniority. During the 20th century, this ideal has been increasingly tested as political administrations have come under greater scrutiny and media pressure leading to the appointment and greater prominence of the government spokesmen closely aligned to political leaders. In 1910, the Conservative Party appointed its first press officer, Sir Malcolm Fraser (L'Etang, 2004, p. 50). Those identified as key names in this development that has been portrayed as the emergence of the 'spin doctor' (a term insufficiently analyzed, being largely a term of abuse) include Joseph Ball (working for Neville Chamberlain), Francis Williams (working for Clement Attlee), Joe Haines and David Kingsley (working for Harold Wilson), Bernard Ingham (working for Margaret Thatcher), Peter Mandelson – known as 'The Prince of Darkness' (working for Neil Kinnock and New Labour), Alistair Campbell (working for Tony Blair) and Andy Coulson (working for the Conservative Party). (It appears that the political domain remains a male province in contrast to the bulk of PR practice.) Questions have also been raised as to the implications for democratic practice of the appointment and access of 'political advisers', and the role of think tanks in opinion and policy formation. These communicative and networking practices may not self-identify or be identified as 'public relations' but are clearly a significant first cousin that should be incorporated within the scope of British PR history.

DOI: 10.1057/9781137427519.0014

Democratization and social change: public administration, local government and democratic education

Of central importance to the emergence of PR in a British context was the extensive political and social legislation passed from the 1830s onwards that forced a profound change in the relationship between government and the governing classes and people, foregrounding the significance of public opinion. Unions, activists and social philanthropists advocated for social changes that supported further democratization. Hence it was Britain's politically neutral public servants who began to discuss the subject of PR, evidenced by a series of articles throughout the 1920s and 1930s in the *Journal of Public Administration* (established in 1922).

The emergence of the idea of professional management in government in the 1920s and 1930s was important in both central and local government spheres in relation to public communication. The arrival of film as a mass communication technology facilitated the development of the British Documentary Movement, led by John Grierson, which endeavoured to educate and celebrate the broad populace so as to facilitate an informed democracy. Grierson's publicly funded films (based initially in the General Post Office (GPO) Film Unit, then in the Crown Film Unit and later transferred to the COI) were inspired by commitment to the necessity for 'public persuasion' (L'Etang, 1999a) influenced by Walter Lippmann and facilitated by the patronage of civil servant Sir Stephen Tallents (the first President of the IPR 1948–1949) who, when the two men met in 1927, was secretary of the Empire Marketing Board, an organization of which it was claimed 'our task is not to glorify the power of the Empire but to make it live as a society for mutual help' (L'Etang, 2004, p. 35; Anthony, 2012). Tallents' ideas inspired a national cultural diplomacy programme, first expressed in his pamphlet *The Projection of England* published in 1923 and which became the blueprint for The British Council formed in 1934 (L'Etang, 2004, p. 36). Thus the overlap between PR and public and cultural diplomacy was a consequence of historical events and the sharing of ideas about promotion and relationships within governmental, political and corporate circles.

The public sector played a key role in the emergence of PR as an organized occupational group in Britain. The local government trade union, NALGO (National Association for Local Government Officers) was founded in 1905 to advocate for rights comparable to central

DOI: 10.1057/9781137427519.0014

government civil servants engaging in lobbying and media relations, eventually formulating a multi-faceted PR campaign from 1932 onwards (L'Etang, 2004, p. 22). NALGO became both a test-bed and a nursery for PR concepts. When local government created communication activities during and after World War II for community and 'general' PR, it was this cadre who conceived the idea of a professional body and possessed the administrative skills to set it up.

Corporate PR

Ideology and politics shaped the emergence of corporate PR in relation to the scope of the free market, trading blocs, nationalization and denationalization and unionization. In the early part of the century corporate PR practices were strongly influenced by advertising and, in particular, by Charles Higham and William Crawford whose visionary approach encompassed public education, advocacy and nationalism (ibid., pp. 51–52). The earliest identifiable PR appointments outside government were in utilities and transport, for example Sir John Elliot (Chairman of London Transport in the 1960s) moved from journalism (*Evening Standard*) to Southern Railways to what he believed was 'the first public relations appointment in Britain' in 1924 (Elliot, 1956, cited in L'Etang, 2004, p. 55). Other organizations that established similar posts between the World War I and World War II were the Gas, Light and Coke Company, Imperial Chemical Industries (ICI), British Overseas Airways Corporation (BOAC), Shell, J. Lyons and Co., Ford Motor Company, Rootes Motors and Brooklands Racing Track (Gillman, 1978, cited in L'Etang, 2004, p. 55).

Lobbying became established as part of PR practice as Watney and Powell was set up in 1926 (though political lobbying pre-dated this as shown by the example of Charles Weller Kent in 1913 (McGrath, 2010)). Financial PR was also evident as early as the 1930s, recalled in detail in Theo Lovell's autobiographical articles published in the *IPR Journal* in the late 1960s (L'Etang, 2004).

Miller and Dinan (2008) interpret the historical evolution of the PR occupation as part of a backlash from corporate and political elites to democratic advancement. They drew attention to the development of business leagues in the earlier 20th century and in particular to the newspaper proprietor, Dudley Docker, who saw politics as a way of advancing corporate advantage since business leagues could form 'a government within a government', an inner circle of influence realized in a variety of propaganda and lobby groups such as the Federation of British Industries (later Confederation of British Industry), the British Manufacturers Association (later the National Union of Manufacturer) in 1915 (Miller and Dinan, 2008, p. 45). In 1942, the organization Aims of Industry was formed by Lord Perry, Chairman of Ford, and relied on,

> The old boy network... linking individuals of varying degrees of weight and influence on the shaping of public affairs... Major attention was paid to the development of 'selective propaganda' ... the whispering campaign technique was a speciality... The organisation of specialist circles for feeding and distributing news and information... feeding selecting writers and journalists with carefully chosen material... the cultivation, socially of a wide circle of journalists, publicists, advertising executives and other PR influences was ... an essential part of the mechanics.... (Kisch, 1964, cited in L'Etang, 2004, p. 86)

The emergence of private-sector specialist consultancies was partially facilitated by advertising agencies diversifying in the face of increased competition and a broadening understanding of the varied nature of marketing and communications activities in the context of debates about the role of propaganda.

The gradual recovery of the British economy in the 1960s and the manufacturing of consumer goods that exploited technological advances made in wartime developed new markets for domestic goods. PR offered secretarial and administrative roles, and the lack of career structure or professional status favoured the advance of women in the 1960s' consumer markets where it was thought that they would be better qualified in terms of expertise and authenticity (L'Etang, 2015a, forthcoming).

Colonial and postcolonial connections: from Empire to Commonwealth

In the relationship with its colonies, Britain took a less-interventionist 'indirect rule' approach in which traditional rulers operated within a British framework (Chamberlain, 1999, pp. 70–71). This required good relations between British administrators and the indigenous representatives despite racism, injustices and under-investment in development and services such as health. Cultural diplomacy embodied by the work of The British Council was part of the strategy to encourage colonial peoples to

DOI: 10.1057/9781137427519.0014

identify with Britain and to build long-term relationships across successive generations pre and postcolonial. This became more important as independence became a more strongly articulated goal.

Decolonization entailed propaganda, information, intelligence and in some cases psychological warfare; PR practitioners were involved in assisting new information structures sometimes based on British models and new national identities, their symbolic representations and realization in national airlines and tourism industries (L 'Etang, 2004; L'Etang and Muruli, 2004). Companies based in countries that were decolonizing, or likely to decolonize, invested in PR to establish congenial postcolonial operating conditions. Decolonization also opened market opportunities for British practitioners to advise overseas governments, a development that in some cases was controversial. For example, Toby O'Brien who had worked for Conservative Central Office was a supporter of Franco from the start of the Spanish Civil War and of Salazar in Portugal and took on accounts to promote Spanish tourism and to act as PR officer to the Portuguese embassy in the UK during the Angolan troubles although he turned down an account for Yugoslavia because he 'didn't like Commies'; Malcolm Fraser worked for the Greek Colonels and claimed he could procure the services of a Labour MP to work for them in Parliament; IPR founder member Lex Hornsby worked for the East German government but claimed 'none of it is political' because the account was concerned with trade, industry, cultural activities and tourism (West, 1963, p. 79; Kisch, 1964, p. 78; L'Etang, 2004, p. 153). Other examples include Sydney Wynne, the son-in-law of Labour politician Ernest Bevin, who represented Sir Roy Welensky's Central African Federation; Pat Dolan who worked for the Obafemi Awolowo, Premier of Western Nigeria; Michael O'Shaunghgun who worked for President Senghor of Senegal; Michael Rice who worked for the Egyptian Ministry of Culture and National Guidance and the Arab League; Condor Public Relations which worked for Federal Republic of Cameroon; and Sam Cotton and Mike Williams-Thompson who worked for Zambian President Kenneth Kaunda (L'Etang, 2004, pp. 153–154).

The 'professional project'

The phrase 'professional project' comes from the literature on professionalism (Abbott, 1988) and explains the energy that drives an occupation from a collection of individuals towards a collective enterprise. Occupations aspiring to professional status seek boundaries (qualifications), underpinning knowledge, social legitimacy; the latter is particularly challenging for PR partly because of its relationship with propaganda, but also because of a reputation for producing 'charlatans' who knew nothing and spent their time hobnobbing in pubs and clubs drinking 'gin and tonic' – indeed allegedly there were some who 'could not open their mouths without opening a bottle of champagne first' (Eden-Green, 1961, cited in L'Etang, 2004, p. 140). The project's origins can be found in the activities of local government administrators responsible for communicating changes in social legislation from the early 20th-century onwards, with increased specialized communication posts being established at an early stage of post-war reconstruction.

The professional project commenced with the formation of the Institute of Public Relations (IPR) in 1948 and its mission for educational qualifications. The IPR Diploma and Certificate were established in 1957, but at the end of the 1960s the Institute devolved responsibility for education to a registered trust Communications, Advertising and Marketing Education Foundation (CAM) (L'Etang, 2004; 1999b). The first person to gain the CAM Diploma was the prominent PR author Frank Jefkins in 1971 (L'Etang, 2004, 1999b). The first university degree was Stirling University's postgraduate degree in 1988; the first undergraduate degrees were set up a year later at Leeds Polytechnic (later Leeds Metropolitan University, now Leeds Beckett University), the Dorset Institute (now Bournemouth University) and the College of St Mark and St John (now University of St Mark and St John) all in 1989 (L'Etang, 2004, 1999b). The number of qualifications at undergraduate and postgraduate level rapidly expanded almost entirely at polytechnics or ex-polytechnics and colleges (Stirling and Cardiff being exceptions). This made sense in terms of vocationally orientated qualifications but was an inhibiting factor in terms of the development of research and doctoral level studies. For many years most people teaching PR in Britain did not have a PhD, many did not have a Master's, some from practice did not have an undergraduate degree.

The political, economic and socio-cultural context of the late 1940s and early 1950s shaped a practice that was focused on notions of 'taste' and 'manners' and notions of 'gentlemanly' behaviour that characterized a staid notion of British-ness that eschewed emotional display (L'Etang, 2004; Cook, 2014). Consequently 'stunts' of the sort that were more common in advertising agencies were somewhat decried and many letters in the *IPR Journal* debated whether publicity was in good or bad taste, generally arguing that publicity and publicity agents were not the same as PR and that consequently publicity agents should be excluded from membership from the IPR (L'Etang, 2004). According to discussions in *IPR Journal* in the 1940s and early 1950s, practitioners were supposed to be quiet, behind-the-scenes operators, partly perhaps in response to the 1948 Royal Commission on the Press which not only drew attention to the absence of a code of practice, specifically in the area of government information where it was suggested that PR offices should avoid 'boosting their own Departments' (Hess, 1948, cited in L'Etang, 2004, p. 161).

The post-war era was marked by a struggling economy (Britain ended the war as the world's largest debtor nation) and the gradual slide into the Cold War, the ideological nature of which profoundly affected the discourse of early practitioners in the IPR. PR was seen as a 'bulwark' against propaganda, the occupation that was of 'un-estimable importance to the world' (L'Etang, 2004, pp. 67–71). It was a time of idealism and hope that the practice could be established as a profession supported by qualifications and theory. The IPR set up its own qualifications in 1957 and a code of practice followed in 1964 (although Basil Clarke had written what became the blueprint for the IPR code for his company Editorial Services in his 1920s *Little White Book*) (L'Etang, 2004, p. 159).

Anti-PR: from The Society for the Discouragement of Public Relations to Spinwatch

Opposition to 'the PR system' was evident from the setting-up of the IPR in 1948. Editors expressed concerns about the practice; journalists wrote vituperative items criticizing and ridiculing the new occupation. Despite, or maybe because, 'a good journalist will truffle a press release' (Interview, 1996) and because many journalists moved to PR as salaries were higher and the lifestyle 'more conducive to family life' tensions rose (L'Etang, 2015a forthcoming). A number of well-known prime-time television programmes hosted representatives from PR and the media, including the famous *TWTWTW* (*That Was the Week That Was*). According to editorial and correspondence in *Public Relations*, IPR representatives did not acquit themselves well – which is probably why, more than half a century later, it is impossible to discover the names of

DOI: 10.1057/9781137427519.0014

those who appeared. There was criticism in the House of Commons, Prime Minister Harold Wilson remarking that,

> It is an extremely degrading profession. I think that corruption is too strong a word. It is a rather squalid profession which is developing. (L'Etang, 2004, p. 149)

A clique of elite journalists went so far as to form 'The Society for the Discouragement of Public Relations', a classic British tease since there was no formal membership; it comprised critical wits who socialized in London pubs and wrote acerbic pieces in publications such as *The Spectator*. Key players included journalists Bernard Levin, Katherine Whitehorn and dramatist Michael Frayn; books by West (1964) and Kisch (1963) added further journalistic critique (L'Etang, 2004). This may seem rather trivial were it not that opposition to PR became more vehement among those who perceived it as a force for conservative forces or political–corporate elites. More recent opposition emerged in the formation of Spinwatch by academic critics David Miller and Will Dinan in 2005, whose work is cited in this chapter.

Concluding remarks and towards a new research agenda

This short account can give but a flavour of some of the themes that emerge from a range of historical sources. At the same time, their limits must be acknowledged. There are many yet-to-be-told stories about British PR, for example the histories of activities in the 1960s and 1970s in music, theatre, literary worlds, festivals, fashion and design. Sport has always had its promoters but there have not been historical accounts of key PR players as events and events management emerged as a discrete discipline. Politics has been better served with a number of autobiographical, biographical accounts of different administrations, politicians and their 'spin doctors' – often ex-journalists. Much less is known of corporate, financial and economic PR, or of 'think tanks'.

Although there has been a 'socio-cultural turn' (Edwards and Hodges, 2011) within PR more widely, this has had less impact on historical writing (L'Etang, 2015b forthcoming) and there is considerable potential within the context of British history to take account of gender, race and class, given the colonial and postcolonial experiences.

DOI: 10.1057/9781137427519.0014

It has also been argued that insufficient account has been taken of postmodern approaches to historical work (McKie and Xifra, 2014). This chapter is part of the ongoing work in progress to understand developments in the British context presenting evidence and argument to support particular interpretations. It shows how PR as a distinct practice with aspirations to professionalism was facilitated by conditions in the political economy, ideological debates and international relations. The organized practice emerged from political, governmental and economic elites; however, the stories of proto-public relations, incorporating activism, community action and religion remain largely untold to date.

References

Abbott, A. (1988) *The System of Professions: An Essay on the Division of Expert Labor* (Chicago: University of Chicago Press).

Anthony, S. (2012) *Public Relations and the Making of Modern Britain: Stephen Tallents and the Birth of a Progressive Media Profession* (Manchester: Manchester University Press).

Bailey, R. and Laville, L. (2010) 'Public Relations Education in Britain: A Case History', Paper presented at the First International History of Public Relations Conference, Bournemouth, UK, 8–9 July 2010.

Berendt, D. (2010) 'Bournemouth University: Revealing Historical Evidence of Public Relations Professionalization and Commercialization: The Early History of Public Relations Education at Bournemouth University – Structure, Evolution, People and Curricula', Paper presented at the First International History of Public Relations Conference, Bournemouth, UK, 8–9 July 2010.

Chamberlain, M. (1999) *Decolonization* (Oxford: Blackwell).

Clarke, A. (1969) 'The Life and Times of Sir Basil Clarke – PR Pioneer', *Public Relations*, 22(2), 9.

Cook, H. (2014) 'From Controlling Emotion to Expressing Feelings in Mid-20th Century England', *Journal of Social History*, 47(3), 627–646.

Croft, R., Hartland, T. and Skinner, H. (2008) 'And Did Those Feet? Getting Medieval England "on-Message"', *Journal of Communication Management* 12(4), 294–304.

Dinan, W. and Miller, D. (eds) (2007) *Thinker, Faker, Sinner, Spy: Corporate PR and the Assault on Democracy* (London: Pluto).

DOI: 10.1057/9781137427519.0014

Eden-Green, A. (1961) 'The Presidential Address: Responsibility to Society', *Public Relations*, 13(4), 31.

Edwards, L. and Hodges, C. (2011) *Public Relations, Society & Culture: Theoretical and Empirical Explorations* (London: Routledge).

Evans, R. (2013) *From the Frontline: The Extraordinary Life of Sir Basil Clarke* (Stroud: The History Press).

Garsten, N. and Howard, J. (2011) 'The Evolution and Significance of Public Relations Specialisms in Contemporary Britain (1985– 2010)', Paper presented at the International History of Public Relations Conference, Bournemouth, UK, 6–7 July 2011.

Gillman, F. C. (1978) 'Public Relations in the United Kingdom prior to 1948' *International Public Relations Review*, 43–50.

Gregory, A. (2011) 'Government and the Dance with Communication: Coming Full Circle in the 21st Century', Paper presented at the International History of Public Relations Conference, Bournemouth, UK, 6–7 July 2011.

Hess, A. (1948) 'Our Aims and Objects', *Public Relations*, 1(1), 8.

Kazmier, L. (2009) 'Leading the World: The Role of Britain and the First World War in Promoting the "Modern Cremation" Movement', *Journal of Social History*, 42(3), 557–579.

Kisch, R. (1964) *The Private Life of Public Relations* (London: McGibbon and Kee).

Kunczik, M. (2014) 'Forgotten Roots of International Public Relations: Attempts of Germany, Great Britain, Czechoslovakia, and Poland to Influence the United States during World War I', in B. St. John III, M. Opdycke Lamme and J. L'Etang (eds) *Pathways to Public Relations: Histories of Practice and Profession* (London: Routledge).

L 'Etang, J. (1994) 'Public Relations and Corporate Social Responsibility: Issues Arising', *Journal of Business Ethics*, 13(2), 111–123.

L'Etang, J. (1998) 'State Propaganda and Bureaucratic Intelligence: The Creation of Public Relations in 20th Century Britain', *Public Relations Review*, 24(2), 413–441.

L'Etang, J., (1999a) 'John Grierson and the Public Relations Industry in Britain', *Screening the Past: An International Electronic Journal of Visual Media and History*, ISSN 1328-975.

L'Etang, J. (1999b) 'Public Relations Education in Britain: an Historical Review in the Context of Professionalization', *Public Relations Review*, 25(3), 261–290.

DOI: 10.1057/9781137427519.0014

L'Etang, J. (2004) *Public Relations in Britain: A History of Professional Practice in the 20th Century* (Mahwah, NJ: Lawrence Erlbaum).

L'Etang, J. (2011) 'Public Relations and Marketing: Ethical Issues and Professional Practice in Society', in G. Cheney, S. May and D. Munshi (eds) *International Communication Handbook of Communication Ethics* (New York: Routledge).

L'Etang, J. (in press, forthcoming 2015a) '"It's Always Been a Sexless Trade"; "It's Clean Work"; "There's Very Little Velvet Curtain": "Gender and Public Relations in Post-Second War Britain"', *Journal of Communication Management*.

L'Etang, J. (forthcoming 2015b) 'Historical Path or Aporia? Historiographical Reflections', in T. Watson (ed.) *Perspectives on Public Relations Historiography and Historical Theorization* (London: Palgrave Macmillan).

L'Etang, J. and Muruli, G. (2004) 'Public Relations, Decolonisation and Democracy: The Case of Kenya', in D. Tilson and E. Alozie (eds) *Toward the Common Good: Perspectives in International Public Relations* (Boston: Allyn and Bacon).

L'Etang, J. and Pieczka, M. (1996) 'Public Relations Education', in J. L'Etang and M. Pieczka (eds) *Critical Perspectives on Public Relations* (International Thomson Business Press: London).

Logan, N. (2014) 'Corporate Voice and Ideology: An Alternate Approach to Understanding Public Relations History', *Public Relations Review*, 40(4), 661–668.

McGrath, C. (2010) 'Charles Weller Kent: The UK's First "Parliamentary Lobbyist" (1913– 1916)?' Paper presented at the First International History of Public Relations Conference, Bournemouth, UK, 8–9 July 2010.

McGrath, C. (2011) 'Early Journalistic and Parliamentary References to "Lobbying" and "Lobbyist" in the UK', Paper presented at the International History of Public Relations Conference, Bournemouth, UK, 6–7 July 2011.

McKie, D. and Xifra, J. (2014) 'Resourcing the Next Stages in PR History Research: The Case for Historiography', *Public Relations Review*, 40(4), 669–675.

Miller, D. and Dinan, W. (2008) A *Century of Spin: How Public Relations Became the Cutting Edge of Corporate Power* (London: Pluto).

Moore, S. (2014) 'Building Certainty in Uncertain Ties: The Construction of Communication by Early Medieval Politics', in

DOI: 10.1057/9781137427519.0014

B. St. John III, M. Opdycke Lamme and J. L'Etang (eds) *Pathways to Public Relations: Histories of Practice and Profession* (London: Routledge).

Norris, R. (2002) 'Communication and Power in Early Modern England: A New Model', *Journal of Communication Management*, 6(4), 340–350.

Pieczka, M. and L'Etang, J. (2001) 'Public Relations and the Question of Professionalism', in R. Heath (ed.) *Handbook of Public Relations* (Thousand Oaks, CA: Sage).

Pieczka, M. and L'Etang, J. (2006) 'Public Relations and the Question of Professionalism', in J. L'Etang and M. Pieczka (eds) *Public Relations: Critical Debates and Contemporary Practice* (Mahwah, NJ: Lawrence Erlbaum).

Rice, C. and Somerville, I. (2013) 'Power-Sharing and Political Public Relations: Government–Press Relationships in Northern Ireland's Developing Democratic Institutions', *Public Relations Review*, 39(4), 293–302.

Somerville, I. and Kirby, S. (2013) 'Public Relations and the Northern Ireland Peace Process: Dissemination, Reconciliation and the "Good Friday Agreement" Referendum Campaign', *Public Relations Inquiry*, 1(3), 231–255.

Watson, T. (2008) 'Creating the Cult of a Saint: Communication Strategies in 10th Century England', *Public Relations Review*, 34(1) 19–24.

Watson, T. (2011) 'The Evolution of Evaluation – the Accelerating March towards the Measurement of Public Relations Effectiveness', Paper presented at the International History of Public Relations Conference, Bournemouth, UK, July 6–7, 2011.

West, R. (1963) *PR the Fifth Estate* (London: Mayflower Books).

Yaxley, H. M. L. (2013) 'Career Experiences of Women in British Public Relations (1970–1989)', *Public Relations Review*, 39(2), 156–165.

DOI: 10.1057/9781137427519.0014

Index

DOI: 10.1057/9781137427519.0015

health communications, 114, 125, 126
HGPR (Het Nederlands Genootschap
  Public Relations en Voorlichting),
  95, 101
Hill & Knowlton, 2, 63, 65, 110, 142
historiography, historiographical, 3, 44,
  45, 46, 89, 124, 152
HPRA (Hellenic Public Relations
  Association), 62, 64, 66, 67

'image culture', 81, 82
image management, 28, 82, 93, 102
industrialization, 94
information (dissemination), 12, 13, 14,
  20, 25, 27, 30, 46, 47, 78, 89, 92, 93,
  95, 98, 100, 113, 148
Information Men (Tiedousmiehet),
  28, 29
institutionalization, 49, 55, 75, 85, 89,
  128
Institutio per le Relazioni Pubbliche, 78
integrated communications, 34, 84
internal communications, 41, 50, 68,
  78, 80, 132
International History of Public
  Relations Conference, 141
internationalization, 47
international PR firms/agencies
  PR firms, 2, 7, 37, 63, 65, 71, 76, 85,
  96, 110, 132, 133
  See Burson Marsteller, 2, 63, 65, 110,
  132, 133
  See Hill & Knowlton, 2, 63, 65, 110, 142
  See Ketchum, 65, 76
  See Ogilvy, 63
  See Porter Novelli, 37
  See Weber Shandwick, 37, 82, 133
Internet, 47, 54, 102, 110
IoC (Institute of Communication),
  64, 71
IPR (Institute of Public Relations), 63,
  141, 142, 149, 150
IPRA (International Public Relations
  Association), 9, 37, 62, 63, 64, 65,
  66, 71, 96, 120, 129
IPRA Code of Athens, 37, 63, 70, 81

ISB Information Service Branch, 6
issue management, 92
Ivy L. Lee, 36, 65, 143

Joaquín Maestre, 2, 127, 128
journalism, journalist, 6, 8, 9, 10, 11, 13,
  14, 23, 27, 32, 38, 39, 53, 55, 67, 94,
  95, 97, 98, 119, 139, 142, 146, 150

Ketchum, 65, 76
Krupp, 50

Law 150/2000, 84
Law on Public Information, 101
legitimization, 32, 149
literary bureau, 49
Literat, 50
lobbying, 99, 113, 115, 116, 142, 146, 147
Logeion, 95, 101
Lucien Matrat, 34, 63, 65, 70, 127

male/masculine/men, 69, 109, 144
management perspective, 97
Mani Pulite (Clean Hands), 83
Manos Pavlidis, 61, 63, 64, 65
marketing, 10, 21, 67, 69, 71, 94, 132, 143
Marseille Speech, 40
Marshall Plan, 2, 34, 64, 76, 92, 125
measurement and evaluation, 55, 68,
  99, 115
media, 41, 51, 55
media (press) relations, 8, 12, 13, 23, 33,
  36, 47, 51, 52, 66, 84, 92, 95, 100,
  108, 109, 131
Michelin, 34, 35
military junta, 61, 63, 148

NALGO, 145, 146
National Information Bureau, 108
Nazi, 2, 44, 47, 51
negotiation, 92
networks, networking, 48, 78, 96,
  144, 147
news bureaux, 23, 49
newspapers, 48, 49
North American, 32, 36, 65, 93

DOI: 10.1057/9781137427519.0015

DOI: 10.1057/9781137427519.0015

UNAP (National Union of Press
    Agents), 37
United States; US, 5, 21, 29, 34, 36, 46,
    61, 64, 65, 66, 70, 71, 93, 95, 118, 119
United States Information Service, 2,
    6, 77, 78
US Army, 6
US model (of practice), 3, 47, 52

voorlichting, voorlichters, 2, 91, 92, 98,
    100, 102

VTK (State Information Bureau), 22,
    23, 24
VTL (State Information Office), 24,
    26, 27

women, 29, 111, 147
World PR Festival, 85
World War I, 46, 48
World War II, 2, 3, 5, 6, 19, 20, 34, 35,
    36, 45, 61, 93, 95, 97, 101, 108, 118,
    125

CPSIA information can be obtained at www.ICGtesting.com
Printed in the USA
LVOW07*0205191215

467212LV00004B/23/P

DATE DUE	RETURNED